The Body of Brooklyn

sightline books

The Iowa Series in Literary Nonfiction

Patricia Hampl & Carl H. Klaus, series editors

David Lazar
The Body of Brooklyn

University of Iowa Press ψ Iowa City

University of Iowa Press, Iowa City 52242
Copyright © 2003 by David Lazar
Printed in the United States of America
Design by Richard Hendel
http://www.uiowa.edu/uiowapress

The publication of this book was generously supported
by the University of Iowa Foundation.

Printed on acid-free paper

Library of Congress
Cataloging-in-Publication Data
Lazar, David, 1957–
    The body of Brooklyn / David Lazar.
        p.   cm.—(Sightline books)
    ISBN 0-87745-845-6 (cloth)
        1. Lazar, David, 1957– —Childhood and youth—
    Anecdotes.   2. Jewish children—New York (State)—
    New York—Biography.   3. Jews—New York (State)—
    New York—Biography.   4. Brooklyn (New York, N.Y.)—
    Biography.   I. Title.   II. Series.
F128.9.J5 L39 2003
974.7'23004924'0092—dc21
[B]   2002075078

03 04 05 06 07 C 5 4 3 2 1

FOR LEO LAZAR AND JOHN WATERMAN

AND IN MEMORY OF RHODA LAZAR

the body of brooklyn

I carry the place around the world in my heart,
but sometimes I try to shake it off in my dreams.
— *F. Scott Fitzgerald on New York*

"I know a place across the Brooklyn Bridge where
they'll never find us."
"What's that?"
"Brooklyn."
— *from* On the Town, *1949*

Is not Brooklyn the City of Churches?
— *Delmore Schwartz, "In Dreams Begin Responsibilities"*

Contents

Acknowledgments

I wish to thank and acknowledge the following publications, in which some of these essays first appeared: *Southwest Review*, "Movies Are a Mother to Me," "Further Father: Remembering John Waterman" (reprinted in *The Anchor Essay Annual, The Best of '98*), and "White Car"; *Chelsea*, "Some Images: Toward a Photographic Mishnah"; *Quarterly West*, "Melon Man"; *Seattle Review*, "Season of Love"; *Houston Chronicle*, "Rear Windows"; *Culturefront*, "My Little Heroes"; *Laurel Review*, "Grottoes: Memories of Christaphobia"; *Gulf Coast*, "Distant Voice"; and *SPOT*, Houston Center for Photography, "Family Snaps."

"White Car" and "Further Father: Remembering John Waterman" were named "Notable Essays of the Year" by *Best American Essays* in 1994 and 1998, respectively.

In addition, I would like to thank the following people for their support of my work: Tom Andrews, Robert Atwan, Cathleen Calbert, Bettie Cartwright, Joan Connor, Ken Daley, George Hartley, Delmore Lorenzo Huber Lazar, Leo Lazar, Marcy Zell Lazar, Roz Lazar, Scott Lazar, Phillip Lopate, Kasia Marciniak, Martin McGovern, Robert Miklitsch, Ann Qualls, Tony Sanders, Devorah Silberstein, Willard Spiegelman, Kamil Turowski, Lois Zamora, and Stephen Zamora.

Special thanks to Whitney Huber Lazar for . . . everything.

A big thanks, too, to my students for keeping me on my toes in Essayland, just down the block from Roseland.

Introduction

An autobiography is a book a person writes about his own life and it is usually full of all sorts of boring details. This is not an autobiography.
— *Roald Dahl,* Boy

I experienced the autobiographical imperative early. When I was in sixth grade, I began an autobiography that I recall getting thirty pages of written (writ large, of course, with crayon). It was called "Who, Me?" and its thematic center was the proposition that I was always getting unfairly blamed. The title carried with it the image of a precocious homunculus pointing a finger to his chest, a look of perplexed but sagacious disbelief on his face that he had been chastised unfairly for some infraction, the mistake the crucial factor for this accidental malefactor. I was *The Wrong Kid* (Alfred Hitchcock directing Jackie Coogan in a dicey career move). George Orwell may be right that boyhood is the age of disgust, but in my case it was also an age of a self-pitying form of self-absorption. I apparently felt that being wrongly accused defined my life to that point, and set out to document it. Thirty pages is no small feat for an eleven-year-old, and I remember being interrupted by some quotidian affair: homework, holiday, a bout of self-loathing. I wanted to go back to the project, but I couldn't find it. The loss seemed staggering: thirty pages, a lifetime's worth of work, almost. This so deflated me that it ended my budding career as the youngest autobiographer in P.S. 216, or perhaps even Gravesend, or all of Brooklyn.

For years, it's struck me as ironic that my first subject should prove so enduring, at least to me. But it wasn't until the throttle of irony was, or I felt was, under my control that I attempted to write essays that essayed myself. Having been a stranger to a romantic self-love, I was surprised to discover that I was as occasionally amusing a companion as I had only allowed myself to suspect in glimmers, and I turned toward myself in a "Where have you been all my life" gesture that I had seen previously only on the face of William Powell.

Autobiographical essays are like vanity film projects, at least to this extent: produced by, directed by, written by, from an idea by, starring. However: costarring Irony. Ultimately it is the way that irony and sentiment, a stern eye, and even a cold eye, and then a resistance to resistance to sentiment, create autobiographical essays that earns their insights. A book of autobiographical essays without irony is like a swimmer without sunblock. Too much uninhibited exposure. The water may feel good, but it simply can't save you. Especially if you're at the end of your metaphorical tether.

Writing personal essays has always felt like a kind of slapstick to me, formally. (I'm incorrigible.) I aver this (I've always gotten the same shiver from saying "aver" as I have from watching Hedy Lamarr smoke — it seems so sophisticated) even when the subject is serious, perhaps especially so. Ironically, even the most dedicated egoist can only stay at the center of his or her universe (personal essayist of the year: Mr. or Ms. Universe!) for so long without some form of deflation being introduced or forcing itself upon the consciousness of the writer. It's the role of the essayist to throw the banana peel down and then dutifully walk over it and pratfall. This may or may not be funny. It depends upon how hard you fall and where you go when you get up.

I have an autobiographical wonderland in my mind, *literarywise* (as Jack Lemmon in *The Apartment* might say), my own private synesthetic Atlantis. It's from here that I aim my quiver, writing as a shot in the dark — though we can aim in the dark, too. Here's a version of a tone I'd love to have: some Mark Rothko, a bit of Red Grooms, a dash of Eric Fischl, and a touch of Cindy Sherman. The score is by Joni Mitchell and Stephin Merritt, with riffs of John Fahey, Bach, Randy Newman. Does it sound like Janáček on acid? The director is Preston Sturges, and the star is played by both Eddie Bracken and John Garfield, the way Buñuel divided his actresses in *That Obscure Object of Desire*. They move through a shifting three-dimensional canvas. That would be magical beyond my means, pretty to think about, and perhaps too crowded. And any list like this risks sounding show-offy: look what I know. I'll now cross my eyes and exit stage right.

But let me know how I've done, will you?

The Body of Brooklyn

White Car

f I could stop that car, see what was inside it. When I was young, I used to indulge in a fantasy borrowed from *The Twilight Zone* (or was it *The Outer Limits?*). I still go into it involuntarily sometimes, but shake it off guiltily. I am in a room full of people, a party, an auditorium, on the street. I can stop time, and in so doing all movement, all but my own, that is. I wander around the still bodies, looking into the frozen eyes, browsing through the cabinets; the inanimate world yields to my manipulations. But I never touch any flesh. It is a voyeuristic fantasy. However, there are no salacious scenes; there is no dramatic process. Simply a frozen tableau. But there *is* great drama in it, in the small gestures, expressions, postures, stopped in their specific inflections. It is a fantasy of complete social comfort, since this is the only social scenario I can imagine that is completely safe. Sure, it's sterile. But also fascinating. What great power I have, to do such a thing! But the power contains its undoing. To freeze I must also restore, and to restore is to return myself to a general sense of social discomfort, if not ubiquitous powerlessness.

Memory, too, is the stopping of time, a process of wax coating, lamination. Bronzing. We look back attempting to turn complicated, fluid events into photographs, heavy with specific emotion. In so doing, memory turns static, atrophies into comprehensibility as we weary of interpretation, the shifting selection of detail. In memory, we urgently seek reconciliation, closure. It is a death wish; it hates the dialectical procedures of remembering, its questions and enigmas. Memory wants to understand, yet stagnates when it understands, settling on a verbal and visual picture. Therefore, photographic memory is nothing to be proud of, especially when the picture is clear. Perhaps only the blurred memory approaches honesty, because within it remembering still lives, shifting and sorting, posing questions that are layered like multiple exposures. Hovering over possibilities is unsettling. And sometimes possibility is all that I want.

When we begin to remember, the memory will not settle. The photographic print is blurred and the negative is lost, but we keep peering closer, shooting for clues we may have missed, trying to make out the figures. We are confronted by the need to interpret in the face of indeterminate images. But we keep circling back as if answers were possible. Finally, in frustration, we resort to words, to locutions, to the anecdote. That language is finite is, at times, a consoling idea. It is a hope against hope, the peaceful promise of tautologies. When language meets its double, it seems to confirm itself. When experience is settled into language, they become twins.

Fraternal or identical? I've never distrusted language before, never seen it as the enemy. I remember The Lady from Shanghai. *If language is a hall of mirrors, it'll do no good to enter with our guns drawn and start shooting. We need to get close to the glass, examine the angles, see which textures are real, and which are reflections, distortions.*

It was July, July in Brooklyn, July in Brooklyn in, say, 1963 or '64. I can never fix my age exactly in this. Summer vacation. Sometimes we went on short trips, to Washington, Philadelphia, Bear Mountain, New Hyde Park. But my brother and I mostly spent our time "around the corner," meaning Manhattan Court. Sometimes we played street games in front of our house, on the service road, a name I never understood. I have always had trouble understanding certain very simple things. When I was about twelve I came across some mews in ... *David Copperfield?* I looked it up, but cognition somehow failed me for years. Perhaps the association of alleys and cats threw me off the scent.

The baby boom had visited our neighborhood with abandon; there were maybe fifteen kids within three blocks, with an age span of six or seven years. I was playing punchball in the street with some friends. Punchball is essentially baseball, played with a Spalding red rubber ball (a "spaldeen" in our lexicon) using one's fist as a bat, self-hitting. We were in front of my house. The rhythm of the games was frequently broken (regulated) by the interruption of passing cars. One started down the street toward us. We instinctively divided, a few on the curbside, a few against the parked cars, and with a nod of the head, street-telepathy, a friend and I agreed to "do the chain."

At a certain point I don't know what actually happened and what usually happened. Much of memory is the extraordinary moment buttressed by a familiar context. How often have you heard someone tell a story that was completely contextual? When it happens, it is usually just a file from the "Way things used to be" folder.

In the chain trick, motivated by umbrage at the disruption of the game, as well as being something to do during time-out, one waits for a car to be right at the border of the game group, and at the shout of "Lift it!" the two players lift an imaginary chain fastened to imaginary objects on the sidewalks, causing the real driver to think that he is about to rip off the better part of his bumper. I suppose, somewhere in Brooklyn, somewhere in the world, they played the chain with a real chain, not the phantom form we indulged in, for the drivers would frequently slam on their brakes, get out, and chase us as we ran for cover, seeking out the hidden corners of the neighborhood. I remember these men (women seemed immune to the bait; perhaps we baited them less frequently) with arms flailing, screaming "Come back here you kids!", the embodiment of Edgar Kennedy. Remember him? Always beleaguered by the Little Rascals, his hand would pull down his face, over his scalp, in frustration.

I was running. In fact sometimes it seems I was always running. Flight was one of my major childhood archetypes. We ran away in all seasons, from any number of pursuers: neighborhood toughs, rival gangs, provoked adults.

We. Sometimes it was just me; other times I was accompanied by a friend, another charter member of the chased-brigade, whose membership was determined by the urge to run away as a first instinct, an automatic response: with the smell of trouble our noses twitched and we turned and were on our way. Cowardice, but it isn't that simple. Running away was frequently a great adventure, a way of confronting the unknown, confronting the unknown by running away. We usually knew what would happen if we were caught. We would be thrashed or admonished, threatened, humiliated. . . . When we ran, we turned certain defeat into a more speculative event. What would happen if we were caught? However, this may have also magnified the consequences out of proportion, kept me locked into the pattern of always trying to escape. Perhaps. But, if only temporarily, it beat the reckoning, evened out uneven odds; to escape was a victory of sorts. Next time was next time.

An alternate view: I was a kid and I ran; I just ran. But I know that isn't the whole story. At times the fear, the excitement, was almost sickening. I think in our minds the punishment for being caught was bound to be incomparably worse than what we were originally facing. Running upped the ante to a potentially cruel and unusual fate. We were running beyond the pale, Cossacks close behind. And who knew what really was beyond the pale? This is essential to the subliminal ideology of running away: the greater the danger, the greater the incentive to escape, and on the heels of that the stimulated wrath of the pursuers, who would rather have done with it, whatever "it" they were pondering. And if the escape was a success, the perverse triumph was accompanied by a real one, the telling and retelling of the story. That was the greatest reward.

The story was our game, and if it was good, a good story always won for me. For example, I used to walk past a dentist's office on my way home from school. It was in an apartment building on the corner of Ocean Parkway, between Brighton Beach Court and Avenue Z. But it had a separate entrance of its own. I had never seen anyone enter or leave that office. Those places that seemed to resist the normal ebbs and flows had a great fascination. Houses where it seemed no one lived, stores that seemed perpetually closed. One time I decided to test the office's existence, pinch it and see if it moved. I rang the bell and disappeared like quicksilver, finding the perfect and time-honored vantage point; I crouched behind a car. Nothing happened. I left. The next day I repeated the ritual with the same results. On the third day, I got my rise. I rang again, but I had been conditioned to safety. I turned laconically, and before I could accelerate, a nurse figure appeared at my elbow, angry and reaching. I felt like a cartoon character, running in air, but managed to get going after what seemed like an eternity hovering.

She was a middle-aged woman, but I had little legs. Well-matched, we kept pace. The thrill of the chase intensified when we ran in front of my house (what would my mother think at the sight of her youngest being chased by a nurse at full throttle?) and around the corner to Manhattan Court. Perhaps getting past the hurdle of my house, my immediate neighbors, and the prospect of open, more neutral ground ahead threw me off. I made a silly error, a novice mistake, as though this were the first chase of my career: I ran around a car stationed in a driveway, forgetting that the victim almost always loses that one. We kept an uneasy balance for a while, the nurse making an arc around the back of the car, which faced the street. She was clearly a street-smart nurse (Had I been lured into this one, a trap? Was the third ring always pounce time?) and would never go so far around so as to give me a shot at my route to freedom, the street and alternative strategies. We caught our breath. I'm tempted to say there was something erotic in the persistence of our eye contact. Finally, she asked, "Why are you ringing the bell all the time? We're an office. Don't you know we're too busy for brats like you?" When cornered, children have a knack for focusing on the legalistic. I remember thinking that "all the time" was a gross exaggeration, and "too busy" an obvious lie. Whether or not it was even a functioning office was in doubt. The combination of these falsehoods shifted the moral ground, as I saw it, but I was in no position to become the Grand Inquisitor. What could I say? Because it was there? I was mute. I shrugged. She pointed her finger at me, making an indentation in my chest through the air: "If I ever catch you doing that again, I'll give you a smack you'll never forget!" And drum up some business.

I was pretty frightened at that point. "I won't," I said. I had no trouble promising, didn't mind backing down, for when caught, a simple strategy always prevailed: do what is necessary to end the confrontation as painlessly as possible. She straightened her hair, stared me down for a moment, turned on her heels, and left. One mystery was resolved, if not solved, but was in time replaced by another: how could I live a block away and never run into her again?

Am I putting a pink ribbon on the story? Wasn't much of my backing off, backing out, backing down humiliating? Sometimes, it was. However, the street has its strata. I didn't back down all the time, didn't back down when I thought I had a chance.

Which wasn't very often. Just often enough, I suppose. When the chances in a confrontation seemed too ludicrously good. One rung below my status were those kids who were so pathetic that no one bothered to chase them. And these were generally the emotionally disturbed class, the type who had nervous ticks by the time they were eight. To be grouped with them was to be avoided with an alacrity exceeding backing down.

Residues, as always: one tends to not face things head on, to look for shortcuts. However, for better or worse, one learns to compensate; I developed speed. You need a strategy when you're weak. And for a long time the world did seem to be chasing me, an outlook that ultimately disarms strategies, dampens triumphs. But I saw different things on the run, on those little lams, and I learned things that would have otherwise escaped my notice, such as how to fit a small body under a bush, or how invisible I could be in a crowd. Or how visible. And the chase was chastening. On the rare occasions when I became the pursuer, I knew that if I won the chase, cornered my opponent, I had to inspire some ignominy. Those times, those elusive few, I wound up running against myself, secretly hoping to be eluded. I would rather have been running away, learning the streets in that other stride, when I learned how to commandeer an elevator, calculate its emptiness when my opponent waited for the door to open on the fifth floor, pouncing on missing prey. I learned how fast I could cover a stretch of asphalt in Hush Puppies. And I learned my neighborhood and the adjacent neighborhoods, the houses, the fences, the cracks in the sidewalk. There is a beauty in the gritty intimacy you can establish with the streets: learning to elude, to not lose. That transformed me, gave me a strategic fast track.

Defensive descriptions of defensive actions. Avoidance, shortcuts, were part of my heritage; they proved cleverness, dexterity, but we knew that standing firm was permanently higher ground. We had been to the movies, and in ourselves there was pathetically little matinee behavior. I am, I realize, far from where I started, and the story I was going to tell.

The car was coming toward us, very fast. The service roads were narrow. It was July, if I remember right, a sultry late afternoon, humid. The heat and long days conspired to make one think that evening would never come, that if it were going to, it should have already arrived and had missed its chance. The car was a white convertible, long, with fins. Buick? Cadillac? That has never been my specialty. Whatever it was was white and raced toward us as we tensed for the chain, but when it was, oh, forty yards away, I dropped the rubber ball I was holding and it dribbled cavalierly into the middle of the street. I stepped toward it, and back, that moment of indecision, like crossing a street in heavy traffic, trying to gauge whether or not you can make it across without getting clipped; you wind up doing a silly two-step, back and forth. Whether protectively or to play a role in the comedy, a friend grabbed me from behind, by the shirt. I turned to him, sensitive to a possible mockery of fraternal concern. "Saved your life," he said, an allusion to the Brooklyn game of pushing someone out into the street while holding on to his shirt, only to pull him back and announce the altruism. At that moment the car whizzed past. I had forgotten the chain in my concern for the ball, which escaped into the trees when the car hit it. My friend on the other side howled in protest at my dereliction, and at that moment I turned and saw the occupants of the car, slightly past profile. What I saw was my father, beaming a smile at a beautiful young woman, a blonde, smiling back at him. I remember it as a blur, but a distinct blur.

How sure am I, was I, that it was my father?

I was not certain, but I was convinced. As for now, I am only certain that I was convinced. I was shocked; I didn't understand. I knew something was wrong, that he should be at work, that for him to be in a car with a young woman was . . . wrong, a betrayal of some kind.

"Betrayal": a strong word for a fleeting glimpse.

I am sure that was not the word I would have or could have used. But writing about the past is the process of turning the immanence of the inarticulate emotion into the falsifying and clarifying vision that is the language of memory. Our speech-memory is hope, a prayer for half-truth.

What did I feel he was betraying? My father was supposed to be at work, not riding around with young women. His role as overworked provider was the axis of the family. It seemed that everything came down to that; we were hit over the head with it constantly. Any infraction, any hint of discord from me or my brother, was treated as a sign that we were incapable of appreciating the sacrifice, the lifelong sacrifice, the sacrifice predating known human history, that he was making three hundred or more days a year, leaving at the crack of dawn, returning late in the evening. All for us, always for us. The sight of my father indulging in such manifestly inappropriate, hedonistic behavior made me feel that I was being cheated on, oppressed by a lie.

Could I have created the scenario, substituted my father for a man in a car, as a way of challenging that burden? A way of undermining my guilt? That isn't to say I blame myself for wanting some relief, some respite from gratitude, but isn't it possible?

I've never really considered that. Everyone is absolved that way: my father is cleared of the half-formed accusations; I am not to blame for betraying him in my memory all these years. Another strategy for avoidance, painless resolution? I distrust the suggestion of my own betrayal; it feels like a betrayal. My father came home at the usual time. Everything was hunky-dory. I imagine I searched for suspicious signs. I don't remember seeing any. I admit that I shy away from equations that seem to dispense with darkness so neatly, just as much as I yearn for clarity.

Perhaps I have held on to the enigma for so long that I've grown accustomed, comfortable with the mystery, even if it sometimes shades into misery. Maybe I had doubts about his fidelity generally: the long hours, the business trips. Maybe the white car was the accretion of doubts I had cued into subconsciously? I just don't know.

Back to betrayal. Did I never think of asking him, after my mother's death, in a moment of casual intimacy, playing "man to man," ask whether he had ever been unfaithful?

No. Why? Call it a concession to family decorum, or a concession to grief, or say there are are boundaries I'm not sure I want to cross. I'd rather hover somewhere between my doubts and the truth. Besides, that would hardly settle it, even if he answered.

So I'd rather not know?

I'm not sure of what is knowable. And in this case I'm not convinced of its importance. If my father drove a white car, with the top down, in Brooklyn, in 1964, I'm not convinced of the case for what I need or needn't know: confirmation of denial, denying confirmation. Perhaps the blur tugs at me more than any answer would.

Just the right number of steps behind? Yes, it promotes a certain psychic pace. So I want something tugging? Or would I prefer for the picture to clear; "We are now returning control of your television set." Do these antipodal desires keep me from ever pushing the focus past a certain point? I do keep looking, but what I see may be permanently out of focus. The white car speeds, what I started by trying to say — not a dream, and not a settled memory. And it never completely stops.

Melon Man

I remember the melon man in terms so impossibly caricatured that his image is indelible. In childhood, not yet jaundiced by experience, our visual taste buds not yet dulled, we see with a clarity that seems exaggerated to the older, larger, more worldly self. In "Such, Such Were the Joys," George Orwell tells us that if he went back to his old school how small it and its inhabitants would seem. Yes, if we were to go back our heroes might shrink, our demons de-demonize, our confusions fade into the depressing process of understanding and categorizing, depressing in the potential of reducing our personal myths with our fears and confusions. How to keep both, how to use memory to enlarge and not dismiss? For one thing: realize what we have lost, acknowledge that we have forgotten even what we seem to remember. Which brings me, for many reasons, to the melon man.

The melon man lived a scant block away, his house on the corner lot of Ocean Parkway and Manhattan Court. In some ways his appearance matched the house perfectly: the front yard was overgrown, unkempt in its creeping vines, rotting leaves, fruit trees half lush and half dead, completely shaded. The house was large, ugly brick and wood slanting in on itself, a fairy tale melange of aesthetic misdirection: a bric-a-brac house, brick and Braque. In memory it is uniformly dark and colorless. Surrounded by an old half-height chain-link fence, the yard would engulf all balls that bounced into its dominion, too scary for even the dared rescue. Our Spalding rubber balls were elastic Grails, one of the most familiar items of my childhood, and yet each almost instantly assumed its own character, its own color, displaying the provenance of its bounces and ricochets, and the relative firmness of its uses: stickball, punchball, stoopball, boxball . . .

The balls that bounced into the melon man's yard were sacrificed, yielded to a surreal landscape of rotting peaches, creepers, and the other detritus that washes up on lots and lawns.

The melon man was very old, bent. Before I knew him as the melon man, a genial name that his appearance belied, he was the old man who lived in the scary house, a dour, rubber-featured entity, always in shabby black suit — the old country look that second-generationers such as myself had lost connection with — stained and faded white shirt buttoned to the top with no tie, floppy big black shoes that seemed never to have strolled, each foot lifted and stamped when he would apparently mimic what the rest of us called walking. He had the largest nose I had, or have, ever seen. It was multidirectional: it sloped and bulged and had a knot at the top and a wart or mole on the side. He was crescent bald, gray splayed hair spraying out the sides, down the back, at different lengths. He must have been sixty-five or so. He was scary, larger than life, yet I could nevertheless perceive something pathetic in his physical demeanor that didn't rankle with his status as goblin, Golem. Children are open-mindedly fanciful, but astute.

There he was in my kitchen, smiling semitoothlessly and nodding his head as I came in. "David, this is Mr. . . . ," and there followed a Polish name, all consonants, which second-generation or beyond children are genetically incapable of pronouncing, or in trying to pronounce turn into bizarrely generic utterances such as "bush-mishnish," trailing off into a whisper. They were sitting at the table eating honeydew. I joined them, the three of us making awkward, squishy sounds with our spoons for a few minutes, sounds that seemed to mimic the melon man's name.

As taught, I started excavating the rind, shoveling the spoon over the small ridges of fruit until all traces of opaque green yielded to white. As the child of Depression-era parents I was instructed to eat everything edible, even if only hypothetically so, on my plate. Gristle, fat, bones sucked dry. And one more scant generation removed from turn-of-the-century pogroms and shtetls, we ate foods that make some of my friends go white in holy gastronomic terror: marrow bones, intestines, brains, lots of liver, salvers of chicken fat the genteel regard as poisonous, for me a legacy of "eat the whole animal," but also, in truth, delicacies I haven't had in years, and dream about.

The melon man was horrified; he stumbled over his blubbery lips to ask what I was doing, less gentle than solicitous, more gentle than admonishing. With uncharacteristic simplicity (when at all threatened by a question, which was virtually always, I could invoke a streak of baroque circumlocution from a strangely early age) I replied, "Eating it all."

"Only eat the fruit, the good part, the sweet part," he said. "I brought your mama these nice melons. Look, there's plenty. You want another piece, have another piece, okay? It's so sweet. Eat what's sweet."

I was suspicious. Adults were not supposed to counsel abandon, even melon abandon, and that's what this seemed like. What to do with this counterpropaganda? Of course, part of me was immediately attracted by the idea. Visions of cornucopias, biblical melon scenes (Were there any? Probably *Song of Solomon*). But all children have their supererogatory superegos, family House Un-American Activities Committees, deeply institutionalized, which question all foreign-seeming practices. The depth of the threat is in direct proportion to the strength of the stultifying injunction it is challenging.

"No thanks, I've had enough. I'm going around the corner now." HUAC adjourned in the face of a standoff.

Since it was July, and the pure enticements of pleasure made so much sense, I decided to cut my conscience to fit this summer's fashion. I didn't realize then that revelations can come full force over what seem like trivial issues, moments. But I felt tremendously upset by the wisdom of the melon man's call to melon hedonism. What if pleasure, symbolically located in melon-colored pulp, in green sweetness, were a more ubiquitous rule of spoon, what if I had been denying simple and available gifts? What if my father had a mean streak? A moist scent of supple, and not at all subtle, appreciations threatened to beckon a monsoon that could overrun the superego-sweeping regulations planted like bulwarks in my desire. In short, what if the pleasure principle was the big one, the godhead of motivations, and denial the dark temptation. The world as I knew it would be turned on its head, all because of the forbidden fruit dispensed by a disheveled man.

The melon man started coming by regularly. Always in shabby white and black with a crumpled bag of fruit, mostly melons, but the occasional crop of cherries. He would say "luscious cherries," sloppily sibilanting every chance he got, as though watery lispings of language were thoughtlessly sensual enterprises, a fricative fricassee. His pronunciation was recognizably first-generation American, though I suspect he was not born here. It had the slight formality, the accentless accent of the professional who struggled hard through mediocre schools and exhausted his achievement when a higher status was in sight, as though being a lawyer were the goal and not the means to improvement. In other words, his diction was proper, but uninteresting unless considered as a specific exemplar of what he was. You know the type of speech, I'm sure: "That is exactly the situation I was discussing previously"; "It was a very amusing experience, all things considered"; "I cannot say I had completely comprehended what the gentleman meant."

Of course, this is all hindsight. My feelings about the melon man continued to explore the narrow ground between unease and discomfort, even after I had settled into my full belief in his position on watching the rind, as opposed to choking on it. I didn't like having this new creature around so much. It seemed as though every time I turned around — no, came in, since he always seemed to have appeared in my absences — every time I flung open the screened storm door, a quick two-step masquerading as wiping my feet, rushing into the house (one returns home as an adult, throws oneself into one's house as a child, supposing the house a desirable place to have returned to), there he was, black crow bending over fruitplate, a slight nod hello with a hint of rubbery smile: somewhere between genial and indifferent. We had the kind of nervous stalemate that gives adolescents nervous tics. I had only one way of looking at this Polish blackbird. He had dispensed, apparently, in the one tiny torrent of megabytes, his one Gnostic truth. So I barely slowed my pace on the way past the kitchen, distinguished from the dining room only by a stroke of the imagination in the kind of arrangements that make row houses geographical wonderlands of the Eastern European order: want to call this Hungary and this Czechoslovakia for a while? Presto change-o, this is this and that is that, because we have said so, and come to think so. Alice in Brooklynland. Alice through the shtetlglass.

As I think back, I find I was quite oblivious to my mother's reactions to the melon man. Since I resented his presence in our dining room, a resentment based on unarticulated mistrust and focused on physiognomy, a resentment, I might add, that would probably have greeted any new human variable in the kitchen, thanks to our almost morbidly nuclear household, I believe I was at pains to give my mother a hard time about the violation of the inner sanctum, and wondered, in a diffuse way, why she was entertaining this tiresome, if clumsily exotic, man. Surely we weren't hurting for fruit money. Twice, three times a week, we would go to the fruit stall in Sheepshead Bay, its awning proclaiming, "I MAY NOT BE A POET, BUT WHEN IT COMES TO FRUITS AND VEGETABLES I KNOW IT." Whatever unfulfilled dreams of ripe Rilkean elegies lay behind the summer squash, or crisp visions of sonnets hidden in the bins holding kale, I merely thought it a non sequitur, but gave it points as an oddity.

In any case, I cast a cold eye at my mother, assuming that she merely hadn't the heart to get rid of him. My mother could be easily imposed upon as long as my father, my brother, and I were not being overtly inconvenienced. And I had no convincing argument to put forth concerning my objections. Discomfort in the kitchen, the truth, apparently never came to mind, perhaps because any "new" adult made me uncomfortable, and I was casually seeking specific objections. He was more an annoyance than a threat, however, so my response stayed short of critical mass, instead took the form of mildly sardonic asides: "Are melons always in season?" Or, "If there were a parallel universe, would we eat can-elopes and honey-don'ts?" Such scorn seemed a proper fate for minor prophets and their accidental impresarios, once the wisdom was exhausted. I simply wasn't quite sure if the melon man was being tolerated out of kindness, a bit sickening but respectable, a lack of assertiveness, despicable in myself and disappointing in my mother, or appreciation, perhaps of some attention or even a whiff of the old country for a young woman with dead parents: incomprehensible to me at the time, but not impossible. The chances are it was a combination of the three, which may seem a safe adjudication, but I have learned not to chase the motivations of my own dead parent beyond psychological necessity. It is bad enough to chase one's own tail without chasing the tail of a ghost; it can disappear most inopportunely.

Around the melon man, then, swirled a certain minor current of uneasiness: my psychological rejection of the father's canonical law, confusion about my mother allowing me to stave off derision, and a near revulsion at this bearer of fruit that exceeded comprehension. Not to mention a growing aversion to anything containing vitamin C.

Then he stopping coming. I noticed the pattern of his absence, not suddenly, since he would appear frequently, but not constantly. I asked my mother what had happened, why he no longer came around. She said, "He was coming over too often, so I had to tell him to stop." I was puzzled, but didn't understand why I was puzzled. It seemed simple enough, and to boot I had an admirable backbone affirmation to plug into my image of my mother, which should have relieved some psychic congestion. Like a narrative Vicks VapoRub. So what was the rub?

The rub was tone. There was an unseasonable mist of dissimulation covering her version of the melon man's departure, as though, close as we had come to autumn, he had not faded into the mellow fruitfulness of eccentric family hangers-on, but had somehow turned bad. That was as close as I got: something not quite right, and not to be pursued. I knew, even then, to let things slide when the openhearted turned away from further explanation.

Orwell says of his school years that he could have remembered them with a finer, more accurate sense of detail if he had written of them sooner, closer to the experience and his earlier self, somewhere between his current middle age and childhood. However, he says, "it can also happen that one's memories grow sharper after a long lapse of time, because one is looking at the past with fresh eyes and can isolate and, as it were, notice facts which previously existed undifferentiated among a mass of others." He speaks of details that "lay unnoticed in my memory." And it occurs to me that unnoticed in my memory was the turning away of my mother, and what that meant. For some reason I know now that the melon man had made a pass at her, perhaps even an aggressive one, and that this was terribly embarrassing, probably because it implied an error of judgment on her part about whom to entertain, to let into the house. I know this; it is not at all a matter of speculation.

The weeds in the melon man's yard grew more tangled, the vines more twisted, if demystified. Which is not to say some mystery didn't remain, dwarfed as it nonetheless was by the restoration of equilibrium: the kitchen liberated. Subsequently, the old man who had apparently wanted to play knickknack with my mother must have made the occasional cameo appearances — nonspeaking walk-ons — in the theater of my childhood; I seem to remember him walking past me, bent and muttering, a few times. I place a paper bag in his hand. I dress him in the same shabby black and white. And then he disappears. And the house on the corner disappears, replaced by newer one-family row houses.

I wonder if my mother ever mentioned the episode to my father. I would guess not, knowing as I do that any conflict, which is to say anything that ever went wrong, never served a higher goal, a greater good, no matter how blameless the one who introduced it, or its irrelevance to other family members. Resolution meant the fight had stopped, someone was no longer mad at someone. I get exhausted just thinking about it, which makes how much I think about it seem somewhat perverse. But I know that in the way my mother turned, she was saying she had something to say which she could not say to anyone. She had no really close friends at the time. My parents did not live hungrily off friendships the way I and much of my generation seem to. Of course, a sentimentalist could argue that she is talking to me now, the communication merely slowed by the space-time continuums of memory and mortality. I am drawn to the idea that we communicate in stages, sometimes decades apart, as gestures coalesce if they haven't congealed, that something said today might light up in twenty years like the light reaching us from distant stars. The lyrical turns elegiac, however, when we consider that the star may no longer exist.

These days I eat my melon to the rind sometimes, partly as a gesture to an old superego who has seen better days, lurking like a cranky beggar rather than a stern schoolmaster, partly in that search for the last sweet spot, the gastronomical diamond that requires mining, but is always something of a disappointment, since one knows that's it, that's all there is, and another piece would be redundant. "Gilding the lily," my mother used to say.

Grottoes: Memories of Christaphobia

New York is Babylon: Brooklyn is the truly Holy City.
— *Christopher Morley*

think I know where, if not precisely when, I first discovered landscape: two grottoes in Brooklyn, by (with? in?) Our Lady of Grace and St. Joseph's Catholic churches. I walked by each frequently. They were always so quiet, well tended, with pine trees and distant statuary on the lawn, forbidden and bidding figures to a Jewish kid raised with the fear of God of the other, especially the goyim-troika and the confusing omnipresence of Mary. In my case it was a strategic mistake, this turning of the cheek toward the other, toward the mystery of their strangely sad gods. Our God, the lawgiver, bestower of somber proclamations, was stalwart, upright, unpained, Talmudically logical (and not uninteresting for this), but certainly not sad. He could invoke neither empathy, since as a child I could not sanction his feelings toward wayward, if chosen, people, nor sympathy: too powerful.

To experience any aspect of the Catholic (difficult to avoid when one's parents committed the strategic mistake of settling in Gambino Territory, Avenue X) was forbidden in profound and mostly unspoken terms, naturally unspoken because to speak would be to admit the existence of the other, as unacknowledged as the statehood of Israel is to the PLO.

Brooklyn was not quiet, Brooklyn was not well tended. There was nothing of Monteverdi and van der Weyden in my Brooklyn. Nothing solemn, nothing classical. It was a messy life full of slush and bodily functions. We lived in the top half of a row house for the first thirteen years of my life, my maternal grandparents in the bottom half. My brother and I shared a small room and designed our cohabitation through opposition. He had a Confederate flag; I bought a Union Jack.

He started listening to jazz. I colonized folk music. Rock and roll was our imperialist's China, divided into areas of interest. (This continued even after we moved downstairs to separate bedrooms. The shared wall was ours, and as though rebelling against the proximate tyranny of our lives, we skirmished for control of it. Phil Ochs would duel with Dizzy Gillespie. I would play Leadbelly records at levels too high to enjoy, and he would come back with Coltrane too loud to endure.) Vanilla and chocolate, Mets and Yankees, tomato and tomahto. Space was a tactically defined commodity: he would bomb me from his residence in the top bunk; I gave him choppy seas with a baseball bat when he most wanted to sleep. Our nights were a fiercely fought doubleheader.

In the mornings, my mother would emerge from a mysterious hour in our bathroom, leaving it almost unbreathably smoky.

My parents' choice of a folding door for their bedroom is extraordinarily anomalous to me, considering their intimacy. It was as though they yielded to a privacy-less existence in a failed stratagem to outwit its impossible equations of space and sound. We were aurally oppressed without knowing it. A murmur from either of the bedrooms, which shared a wall in the back of the house, would carry clearly. That is probably the reason for my adult mania for silence, for not having the sounds of others intrude into my psychically sensitive ears. In my late teens I visited a forum at Pompeii and was treated to the acoustic cliché of hearing a pin drop in the center circle from way up in the bleachers. I was unimpressed. I had heard pins drop all my life.

But the grottoes always seemed supernaturally quiet. Of course, they weren't, technically. They let in as much of Brooklyn as any garden-variety garden. But the space shaped my sense of sound, or rather soundlessness, as though a natural, still life could still noise, as well. The distant Madonna at St. Joseph's, so sensually gentle holding that forbidden child of hers, that lost son of my tribe. Judaism always seemed masculine to me. The women always seemed like a sideshow, with two exceptions. My namesake, David, who I was led to believe took the other sex rather too seriously, and one moment from the Book of Ruth, which I happened to read for some now unfathomable reason, when I was eleven or twelve. I have remembered the line "Rue is for Ruth" since, a line whose comprehension has been forever shadowed by its echo and assonance. Even so, this verbal mystery, built on a story of exile from my close-quartered tradition, did not beckon as compellingly as the albino woman in the quiet garden. Waking up was a family activity. It was simply impossible to remain oblivious to the lights, radio, flushing of toilet, voices. If we lingered in bed fifteen minutes or more after my parents were moving about, my father would stalk into our bedroom and toot an imaginary bugle, as though we were some small and forgotten, some absurdly quartered Jewish regiment.

The grottoes were a young Romantic's dreamscape: an artifact of sublimity with no distractions. I loved them, but couldn't for the life of me figure out what they were. They seemed hushed, and therefore holy. No one was ever in them. I wanted to be in them, not to romp, certainly, not even to read silently, but just to exist in them, be an invisible part of the landscape, to feel their perfect composition, to feel perfectly composed. In the grottoes, existence itself was orgasmically static, almost superfluous, as though one moment of it would be enough for eternity.

On a trip to Jerusalem when I was twelve, I wandered off by myself through the old city. A monk, heavily robed, beckoned me into what I remember as an igloolike structure in the middle of the street. We crawled through the opening, and onward ten yards or so, until we were nowhere recognizable, somewhere in the near darkness, lit only by the single taper this bearded holy man carried. I remember him telling me we were at a station of the cross, which I only vaguely understood. Clearly it had something to do with Jesus Christ. I had been segregated, but I wasn't dopey. But I got stuck on "station." What a strange word to pair with "cross," I thought. The only stations I knew were Penn, Grand Central, the generic stations where we would catch the subway. I could not conjure any picture that would reconcile station and cross, other than a stationary cross. Was this a place where crosses were planted as markers, as a kind of doleful roadway for the soon-to-be crucified? In any event, the monk told me it was a place where Jesus had been. Before I could react, act out my discomfort, he dipped his fingers in holy water and placed them on my forehead, those cool wet fingers. I was horrified; it felt soothing. "I've got to go now," I told him, and started backing out, hunched, as though my entry were being shown in reverse. When I got to the street, I turned and saw him sweetly waving bye-bye. I felt the exhilaration members of my family always seemed to feel when we had a story to tell. When my father later referred to my experience in the grotto — in an attempt to convince me that the holy water had acted as a kind of spot religion remover, rendering me un-Jewish — I bounced back in protest: the cave I had crawled into wasn't a grotto. It was antigrotto, if anything: closed-in, dank, dark. Even years later, my verbal imagination insisted on the earlier, airier definition.

In time I developed a personal relationship with the grottoes that transcended mystery. They seemed to know me, almost to yearn out as much as I was yearning in. True, they were more implacable than I was, but that was only to be expected, metaphysically speaking. It felt as though we were meant to meet at the wrought-iron boundaries. My intuition was informed; I learned that there is a poetry in distances, that yearning could be a higher plane, lightly stimulated by painful borders. The grottoes said, "Come to me, come no farther." I said nothing. I wrapped my palms around the fences.

As a teenager I would play *Jesus Christ Superstar* obsessively, but only in the afternoons, singing all the parts, delighted to act, to sing the prophet, Judas, the rabble, the devoted, with — except for my unacknowledged tie to the grottoes and their undecipherable suggestions — no strings attached. My father would not tolerate this subversiveness, the insinuating note of false messiahs secretly proselytizing through popular culture. However, my mother would never dare intrude on the sanctuary of my music. Besides, she had no power, no prerogative to intercede in the interests of my father, distant and all-powerful (though that power was beginning to weaken). Intercession, we implicitly understood, worked the other way, although in my family it rarely worked.

This mutual devotion, this grotto-love, faded for a while in my late teens when I was overwhelmed by landscapes of women, the beginning of my modern romance with Manhattan, the heart of the heart of the city — as opposed to the grotto-soul — and women in the city. Their hearts. Those quiet places faded. My education poisoned them, elbowing my antiauthoritarianism into revolt, betrayal. The grottoes darkened, a plague of crows hovered on the horizon, flirted with the Pieta, threatening to besmirch. They became the supple kid glove covering an iron fist. I learned about compunction, and unction, and inquisition. And I returned; as we age we learn to slip past our disquietude to the compelling nostalgia for unblemished early symbols. The last time back to Our Lady of Grace, several years ago now, I marveled at how small its garden was, and noticed some patches of dry grass. And as sometimes happens, I thought how ungainly, how disgruntled a word *grotto* was, and how strangely quiet this place was still.

The Body of Brooklyn . . . .

My body lies over the ocean
My body lies over the sea
My body lies over the ocean
Oh, bring back my body to me

This is what I *thought* the lyrics were when I was a boy, when I was an adolescent. This is what I *heard*. The words made sense, a mysterious kind of sense, no doubt, but I understood why the body should be so far away, and why someone might be plaintively calling it back.

Vauvenargues wrote that "the heaviest object in the world is the body of a woman one has ceased to love." Despite the patina of misogyny in this statement, it contains its share of emotional acuity about what we see and when we see it. But I would amend it, slightly: The heaviest object in the world is the body of the self one has ceased to love. I know this because the single greatest determinant in my life has been the fact that I was fat.

If I had a photographic memory, I'd be in trouble. It's bad enough as it is looking at some of the fatty photographs. It isn't even so much the obvious weight itself, which can sometimes be attractive when worn right; no, it's the way I'm bursting out of my clothes, sagging in my body. It's the self-loathing that seeps through the sepia.

For the record: I started getting hefty around five or six. By eight, I was about twenty-five pounds over. By twelve, forty, and by fourteen, sixty. There is a photograph of me in summer camp, the only time I went, aged fourteen. I am standing on a bunk with a sock in my mouth. My stomach peeks through a too-small polo shirt. I had just fractured my hip trying to beat out a weakly hit ground ball to the shortstop. I'm looking at the camera, and my eyes are blazing. As I remember it, I wanted the entire world to die, to combust spontaneously, and actually concentrated my energies at times to see if that would work. Uri Geller had been appearing on the Johnny Carson show, you see. It didn't work. I remained a fat boy who saw himself as nothing short of a freak. And I couldn't even roll a cigarette with my lips and tongue.

Part of the problem was that I never accepted myself as a fat kid. I thought of myself as a victim of a terrible accident, or a mystical act of mischief. I'm not really fat, I wanted to plead. I'm really extremely slender: I match my rapier wit. I knew the point would be lost. Jugular, the evil genie who imprisoned me in the Cave of Lardite, close to the Slough of Despond, never appeared to confirm the theory. Despite my baroque sense of causation, much of this story has familiar dimensions: always chosen last for basketball and baseball, not, I would later learn, because I was so inept — I grew up in a classic sports triad: Dad and the two boys, following box scores, going to games, shooting hoops — but because I completely lacked confidence. I couldn't believe that anyone whose stomach protruded that far could slide into second, or make a layup when guarded by a lither opponent.

Of course, part of the problem was also that I saw myself as metaphysically fat, permanently, essentially bloated. And in many ways still do.

My maternal grandparents lived in the downstairs apartment of our row house. After my grandfather died, for about a year my brother and I alternated spending the nights with our grandmother, sleeping in the same bed, old-world style. There are three things I remember most about Rose, in addition to her general good humor. When I was three or four I enjoyed squeezing her rather ample breasts and shouting "Honk, honk." This amused her to no end. She enjoyed watching wrestling. The wrestlers she approved of, such as Argentina Apollo, would win a winning smile of appreciation and murmuring. To those she disapproved of, apparently because she thought them especially dirty fighters, she would unleash a polyglot torrent of epithets, drawn mostly from Russian and Yiddish, and pantomime spitting three times. My third memory is specific: the day before she died — she had been housebound, out of her mind, for months, due to a series of strokes, and would have long, haranguing conversations with dead relatives, apparently thinking them no better than the lowliest wrestler — her mind cleared, for just moments. My parents, my brother, and I were headed out to dinner. I stopped in to see her; I was wearing a little blue blazer that could barely fit around my stomach. She said hi, surprising me. She had come to think I was a lowly wrestler, too, apparently, or something, at least, that she wanted nowhere near her. I asked her how I looked, but I'm not sure why. She said, "You look swell." I've always remembered that heavily accented "swell," such an American word, a beautiful American word, as Delmore Schwartz would have it. I've wanted nothing more than to look so again, or feel I did, in the thirty-eight years since.

My brother and I were both Randy Newman fans, starting in our early teens. I always identified with Newman's vaudevillian freak-show song, "Davy the Fat Boy." Unfortunately, during times of civil war, my brother associated me with the song as well.

> Davy the Fat Boy
> Davy the Fat Boy
> Isn't he round?
> Isn't he round?
> What do he weigh folks?
> Can you guess what he weighs? . . .
> Win a Teddy Bear for the girlfriend
> Or something for the wife
> You've got to let this fat boy in your life
>
> I think we can persuade him to do
> The famous Fat Boy dance for you
> Give me half a chance
> I just know you'll like my Fat Boy's dance

Once, when I was thirteen or so, we were playing baseball on a lot near Beach Haven, that barely middle class housing development off Avenue Z in Brooklyn built by Fred Trump, Donald's father, who was always referred to, monolithically, as Trump, no doubt because of the enormous cooperative housing development in Brooklyn that still bears his name. (And while I'm here, I must ask a question that has bothered me for some time: certainly wealth has a rather dubious correlation with virtue, but how did Donald Trump, raised amidst splendid wealth, end up so commonly vulgar, so quotidianly boorish, without even the veneer of slick, window-dressed lucre-induced civility?) Sorry: baseball. I couldn't hit for power, but occasionally I'd rap out a well-placed line drive through the middle. It was the eighth inning, tie-score, one out, no one on. I saw a gaping hole between the third baseman and the bag, and since we were hitting fungo, tossing up the ball we would hit ourselves, I angled a sharp grounder at the hole. It worked, and I, what shall we say, plodded full speed around the bases for a triple. Teammates cheered. I had done something for a change. Up next was my pal Sal, whom I would later spend much of high school with, riding aimlessly around Brooklyn until it was time to go to the diner again. Sal was an unusual kid, placed interestingly between the groups, all from the neighborhood and same schools, that coalesced for sports. He was very smart, but not an egghead, and not one of the very top achievers academically. He was as much a wise guy as anybody, but never indulged in cruel ridicule, even though he leaned to the heavily sarcastic. He was tough enough so that no one ever bothered him, but too nice to ever want to prove it, as did those in the asshole brigade. There was something slightly removed about him, just short of mysterious. And he was entirely sensible. To add to this, he could keep one eye still and open, and slowly drop the other lid, like a swarthy, fifteen-year-old Charley McCarthy. For some reason I found this unbearably amusing for fifteen years, and were I to see Sal's performance tomorrow, would be no less amused. Forty-year-old men don't giggle enough, after all. I always admired Sal, because I thought he was the perfect combination without seeming to try for it; there was nothing forced or artificial in his demeanor. He was usually the third or fourth person chosen for a game — not the very best athlete, but you knew he'd deliver and that he had stamina and determination.

And Sal was at the plate. I held my legs wide, one foot on the bag, preparing to tag up should he hit a pop fly. He hit a pop fly to the center fielder, not deep enough for an easy score, but deep enough.

My lumbering body, unused to being the center of athletic drama, sent waves of confusing signals to my mind. I started early. I went back to the bag. The ball was caught, I started again. For some unknown reason I went back to the bag again. Then, as though I were some kind of schizophrenic base runner, I started racing toward home. My body moved in slow motion, as though my legs were singing work songs. The throw to the plate beat me by yards. My teammates rolled their eyes but said nothing. They were flabbergasted. I was in full blush and sick with humiliation. Sal tried to console me on the walk home, saying it was just a game. But the point was that it was just a game and a game was very important and I had blown it, or this lumpen sack of flesh and confusion had. My body had a mind of its own, and it shamed me. And I ultimately deserved it. If I could not establish the First Cause of my fatness, I was still bound to live in its universe, play by its rules, and suffer the consequences, a stranger in a strange body.

I lost control over my body one other time, as dramatically, just shortly after I lost my weight. Bowling. Friday bowling league was one of the highlights of my early to middle teenage years. I was captain of a team — the Knicks, of course, since my family had had season tickets starting in 1968 — at Shell Lanes in Brooklyn, close to Avenue X. My one constant partner was my tautological friend, Rob Steele, and we had one of the only ethnically mixed teams in the league, which was composed of two or three teams of Jewish kids, the rest Italian. Our two other partners varied. One year it was Robert Valle, my next-door neighbor, whose mother was the "second wife" of a mob guy; the next year it was Greg Uzoaga, my close and enigmatic friend, whose father was treasurer of Nigeria and mother was principal of a New York junior high school. Greg, the only black kid in the league, didn't have an easy time. He was subtly taunted, since no one wanted to take him on one to one, and for a very good reason: Greg would have ripped any of them up, tossed them into the air, and watched them float down like confetti with an unqualifiedly satisfied look on his face. Once or twice, at school, I saw him win fights with the toughest kids around, in two seconds flat. And since an ambush by several kids would be inviting a mob scene — remember, this was circa 1969 — Greg gradually became untouchable. He was elegant and quiet and very funny, too, and an occasionally devastating bowler when he cared to be, about one-fifth of the time. But Greg didn't care about much, really.

Greg attempted the same function Sal did, when I lost my bowling bearings. Having just lost my weight, I must have been fifteen or so. One Friday, the third game of three, I had been bowling well. I was rather unpredictable on the lanes, veering from the mediocre to the excellent, depending on whether I got into a groove early. I could bowl

220, striking six times in a row, or I could go two games with nary an X to show for myself. On this Friday, early in February, I ambled down the lane, starting almost from the scoring table, my feet following their precisely calibrated motions. My right arm, holding the ball with my left, took control and gradually started to arc the ball out behind me, and . . . and . . . my body just stopped. It didn't follow through my usual motion. It didn't seem to know what I wanted it to do.

To the laughter of teammates and puzzlement of our opponents, the Jets, I started anew, not having committed any foul that would prevent me from doing so. I aligned my feet at the foot of the alley, began my slow, small, intensely focused steps down, the right hand feeling the swinging weight of the ball, and . . . I stumbled, but didn't fall. And I realized what was happening: I had forgotten my motion. I tried one more time, and my attempt was as grotesque as the first two times had been amusing, at least to the onlookers. My formerly fluid motion had become a tripping, halting progress. I could not try again, and to my teammates' chagrin, and in a deep, and what felt like abiding, sense of humiliation, I left the alley and did the march of shame home, through a February evening, no less. Greg grabbed my arm, hard, as I was gathering my things to leave. He was smiling that Greg smile that meant something which one thought mattered, mattered not at all. He tried to mumble something consoling, something like "Fuck it." But I wasn't at a place where I could learn that most valuable "Fuck it" lesson. Instead, I learned that evening that my body's betrayal was not limited to obese athletic underperformance, not beginning to understand that I was still working with newer, slimmer material that hadn't had much practice in its new form.

I learned something else that night, too. I went home, and spent three hours in my room writing poetry. *That's* how disconsolate I was. It was a completely unpremeditated performance; I had never written poetry before. By the end of the evening, I had written a rather dark and predictably gothic ode to a beautiful young woman who was killed by three friends who knew that her beauty made her an uncapturable object of desire for them. It was ghoulish and adolescent, and not really all that bad. It won a prize, as I recall. Unfortunately, I capped my little lyrical *aristeia* by waking my parents up to show them what I had written. I was clearly excited about what I had written, and I now think of having aroused them with a kind of wincing tenderness; what a madcap move on my part, that desire for a parental blessing for what had been inscribed. *Inscribed*, written out of some deeply threatened place. My having woken them, they gave me a kind of confused approval, and I immediately regretted the sentimentality of my desire to share this new work, this new *thing*, with them. I was embarrassed beyond bowling. The cycle of shame completed itself.

My body was clearly, however, now possessed by aliens, who had stepped in to fill the vacuum left by my not-so-dear departed fat cells. It was as though I had to find a new way to be off balance, off-kilter, off. But I'm jumping way ahead before I've really gotten started.

I was fat, and we lived in Brooklyn, in a gray area you could call Bensonhurst or Gravesend.

I was weaned absurdly late, giving up the bottle at age four, fully toilet trained by age six. On the toilet, I would yell out to mother that I was "finished," and she would come in and wipe my behind. Once, when I was seven, at a beach club on Long Island managed by my uncle Henry, I had to go to the bathroom. Badly. I couldn't or wouldn't or was afraid of going to the men's room alone. My mother gave me permission to shit on the floor of our cabana. I squatted, and the deed was done. She cleaned it and me up. I felt like a squalid cave dweller, like a foul domestic animal, like Hula, our dog, which we brought home from the pet store right around the time I started performing my own bathroom functions; my brother called her Pigdog, and would bring out her favorite pillow when we had parties so she could publicly hump it, causing much merriment all around. Hula was never housetrained. For sixteen years, virtually all of the carpet in our living room was covered with the *New York Times*. Hula would inevitably find the one uncovered spot. My father would inevitably step on the one formerly uncovered spot. He was disgusted; my mother was remorseful; my brother stifled his laughter, lest his hilarity arouse my father's already inflamed temper. I think my level of identification with that dog was too strong to do other than register the scene. I may have, along with Hula, occasionally whimpered.

The body:
The problem was the middle trunk, *media res* me.
It was bloated and it bulged.

I was five feet six inches at the age of fourteen. I wore a size thirty-six *husky*. *Husky* was probably my first experience of the failure of euphemisms meant to make things nicer. I knew I was a size thirty-six *fat*. I had a double chin. My face, larger than it should have been, made my small nose, an anomaly in a family of Jewish Roman noses, look too small. My brother said I had a piggy nose. I remember telling him, in a hollow rhetorical triumph, that I could do something about my weight, but that he would be stuck with his schnozz forever. My father would say, "You would be so handsome if you weren't fat."

The sine qua non of self-hatred: climbing out of the tub and standing on its edge so that I could see my naked body in the medicine cabinet mirror. I squeezed and squeezed the folds of fat of my stomach while looking myself in the eye and saying you are disgusting, you are so disgusting, you are such a disgusting pig, you fat fuck, you disgusting piece of shit.

After most of the weight came off, with a few years of being in the normal range, having courted my first girlfriend successfully, I realized that my change was still not quite dramatic enough. I wanted to be Cary Grant. Of course, even Cary Grant wanted to be Cary Grant, but this did not curb my desire to be attractive, specifically to be attractive to women, which I have sometimes felt was the single most determining impulse of my adult life.

Weight had needed to be lost (passive constructions can be a blessing to those who feel oppressed), but so did accent and whatever else stood between me and the brave new world of attractiveness I may have imagined. It took longer for the accent to drop, but it slowly flattened out. Nevertheless, I clearly had conflicting feelings about what I might be losing. In college, I felt out-Classed, but not outclassed, and part of me resented what I was choosing to do, creating the vaguely Eastern but ultimately unidentifiable accent that has hallmarked my adult speaking life. The bargain struck was to use an exaggerated Brooklyn accent as a "situational" voice: at parties, in fun, for effect, in such a way that it was clear that if not completely Cary Grant — no Judys, and speaking the word "yar" was always out of the question, over the top — then at least I was not immediately recognizable, not easily coded, not Brooklyn, even if I could "do" Brooklyn.

Years of therapy, years of thinness, years of spending time, romantically or sexually, with highly attractive women, have had, in some ways, little effect on my body's mind. One thing I've shared with lovers, women friends: talk about the body, about the extra pound or two, about dieting. I think many men experience such talk as effeminate and don't indulge. This is a shame; anxiety needs company. But, nevertheless, I can't claim that I have ever felt pretty. As Virginia Woolf says, "It is far more difficult to murder a phantom than a reality." And certain memories just won't stay dead.

Names I was called: Chubbsy-ubbsy (from the Little Rascals, I think). Fatty Arbuckle. Sebastian Cabot. Slob. Porky. Pig. I'm not sure how this happened, since I don't believe I ever had especially large or supple breasts, but a few of the neighborhood kids started calling me Brassiere Bizarre, the second word a play on my name. Fatso, which has a kind of classical ring, a familiarity that takes the sting out, except for the fact that you know you really are disgusting.

Songs keep telling me where I was, and when, speaking of and to my body. I remember sitting in the room I shared with my brother, watching him clean, and hearing the opening guitar chords to "Mrs. Brown You've Got a Lovely Daughter" come on the radio. I remember, maybe five years before that, standing under the awning of our row house in Brooklyn and singing "she wore an itsy-bitsy teeny-weeny yellow polka-dot bikini" for my grandparents. They laughed a teeny bit nervously, memories of my desire for a Ken doll swimming in their aged Ukrainian eyes. I think this performance was witnessed by our next-door neighbors, the Shapiros, as well. Our porches were attached, so on many summer nights this elderly German couple would sit out, as would we, both families in friendly disregard of each other. They had a son, Jerry, who would baby-sit for my brother and me on occasion. He would play early rock and roll for us: Chuck Berry, Little Richard, Elvis. Only his binding and gagging my brother and me one rainy afternoon could put a stop to these otherwise pleasant interludes. I remember crying, his pleading for me to stop, the rain, and tearing loose once set free. All the ingredients for a slightly skewed, but not unfamiliar, pop song: "Crying in the Rain." Jerry later stole our bicycles and robbed our house, as well. His mother would wail "Jerry, Jerry, Jerry," at the top of her German lungs, to bring him home. All the ingredients for a modern addition to the Ring cycle: we supplied the ring, several of them in fact. We, my brother and I, used to say that the voice itself drove him to it.

Jerry was a kind of dark, proximate presence, but for balance I had his contemporary, my eight-years-older cousin Lewis in New Jersey. He would spin Janis Joplin and Led Zeppelin records for me and let me peruse his *Playboy* magazines. Janis Joplin and *Playboy*. Raw heartache and idealized rhetoric, a strange and satisfying combination. Lewis's mother caught on to our unashamed endeavors and, astonishingly, gave me a subscription to *Playboy* for Hanukkah. I was delighted and unnerved. There seemed to be tolerant smiles in my immediate family, but no apparent disapproval. Hereafter, I thought, I could choreograph my own afternoons! *Playboy* and Bob Dylan, say, or *Playboy* and Peter, Paul and Mary: a *ménage à quatre*. The initial complication for me was that some time shortly before or after I had acquired quite a reputation for masturbation in my house.

One time, when I was fourteen or so, my father brought home a bag of cosmetics, some reward or bit of barter from his travel business: if my father could secure a difficult reservation on a plane or at a hotel, he would frequently be given goods instead of cash; these varied from dresses for my mother to clothing for my brother and me, tickets to Broadway shows, a couple of dozen steaks, or . . . bags of cosmetics. I stole a small bottle of hand cream from the bag a couple of days later. I was sure in the undifferentiated mass of lotions and creams, shampoos, rinses, bottles and packages whose arcane feminine purposes I could only guess at, that no one would notice a missing vial of generic skin softener, which I thought would provide a nice tactile change from my usual masturbatory lubricant, Noxzema. Noxzema and I had a sometimes affectionate and sometimes changeable relationship. I was always pleased by the smell, faintly medicinal, but clean, bracing, and the slight tingling the "medicated" cream induced was usually fairly pleasant. Call it a low-key masturbatory astringent. There were times, however, if I was on a tear of frequent self-satisfaction, that the Noxzema would tingle almost to a stinging point; I'd start to feel burny. Especially, but not exclusively, at those times (sometimes I simply wanted a change of pace, of sensation) a substitution would have to be found. The bag of cosmetics seemed to provide such an opportunity.

A day or two later, when I was secretively flush with manual bliss, my mother started absently mentioning that a bottle of hand lotion was missing from the cosmetics stash. This low-key conundrum soon spread like wildfire to my father and, most unfortunately, my brother, who seemed to think I did nothing but masturbate (whereas I, conversely, thought he rarely did, or did so with such excessive secrecy that he was perversely private about it) and missed no opportunity to drop little jabs about it around my parents in ways he thought they would never get but that I would be uncomfortable enough to worry about. And this, in fact, was an excellent choice of teenage sibling taunting.

You see, I would be downstairs in our little brick row house, in the small apartmentlike space where my brother and I had our bedrooms, a bathroom right next to mine, and what was for some reason that no one could ever fathom called the playroom, some American dream space of boyhood fun that was mostly used for storage and was dominated by my grandparents' enormous Deco mirror, and my mother would invariably choose the exact time of the day, or times of the day, when I had retired to the bathroom with my *Playboy*s, to need to talk to me. It was unnerving. I would be secure and happy behind a locked door, in the throes of myself, with accompaniment by the low fluorescent hum of the vanity light, the clean smell of Noxzema, furiously fantasizing about some seduction (of *me*, I should add; my fantasies were accurate predictors of my forthcoming sexual life, after The Prostitution Years yielded to the years of wanton passivity — I slept with just about every attractive woman who desired me enough to pursue me), using my mind to use my body to take me out of body, out of Brooklyn, to some antiseptic semitropical living room, some odd combination of palm trees and staid plaid couches where — O Sigmund! — an older woman would be plying me with her wiles, playing me with glimpses of promised lands, forbidden fruit, in fact manna, since I was cooking this pot of dreams out of the free-floating ingredients of desire, when . . . *David! David! David!* One's name announced by one's mother is an aural cold shower. Worse. A cold shower raining shame, since your hand, surfing your cock for pleasure, spills over a

stroke or two, at least, after the announcement of your name and before the slow drumbeat of bare feet descending the carpeted stairs
above your head. Curiously, she would stop at the bottom few stairs,
before they took a carpeted left turn for three more steps to solid carpet (a defecatory brown shag that my brother and I, given our choice,
agreed on in some bizarrely desultory truce). *David!* This one would
usually be singular.

The thing is: I was convinced she knew I was in there. Clearly, my
mother had some sixth sense, some supernatural ability to enter and
disrupt the heart of my masturbatory world, either because she a) disapproved, b) was curious, c) wanted on some level she undoubtedly
did not understand to share this experience, d) some of the above,
e) none of the above. I'm not trying to be speculatively coy; to write
autobiographically is to a) embrace contingency, b) make believe that
one can avoid embracing contingency, c) some combination of the
above.

My mother's voice having voiced my name, what was I to do? I
clearly needed to respond, since she would continue on toward me if I
didn't. She would wonder why I hadn't responded even if we used the
fiction that I was "indisposed" — on the toilet — as an invariable
cover. So, I would usually say, "I'm indisposed, I'll be out in a minute,"
to send my mother out of the realm of my earthly delights, although
for several crucial years I would struggle to try to block out any
thought of her, laboriously, feverishly, if I made the decision to finish
myself off quickly. Perhaps that was when I was first infected with the
fever of words: "mother" winding its way around body parts and epithets, entreaties and almost-satisfied near words, between groan and
articulation.

Indisposed. From Delmore Schwartz to Edward Dahlberg to
Henry Roth to Kate Simon we see a kind of lovely and indispensable
facade of euphemism among first- and second-generation Jewish
Americans, whether it consists of epic Oedipal contortions circling
Dahlberg's mother's body, or Schwartz's "The Beautiful American
Word, Sure." Indisposed. We had, for the first twelve years of my life,
one medium-sized and three smallish rooms for four people. The
bathroom was tiny, and our intestines large with a bizarre combination
of the old country and a brave new world: sweetbreads and TV dinners, gefilte fish and Pop-Tarts, marrow bones — which we would

suck tenderly for that sweet pinhead of rich meat — and pizza. It was a gastronomical league of nations with the United States and the Lower East Side as its Security Council. And, of course, this bizarre combination of culinary customs had to go somewhere, and one outlet was clearly not enough. But the upstairs bathroom — our only one before my grandmother died and the downstairs apartment was liberated as the newly created nation of "our own rooms" for my brother and me — was so frequently occupied, the space so small and intestinal noise so accessible, that a language of denial was necessary. We were indisposed to saying exactly what it was we were doing *in there*. Language, therefore, as a completely lucid method of obfuscation, was introduced to me via my bowels and my Brooklyn culture of thinly veiled politesse. Kundera says, in *The Unbearable Lightness of Being*, that the denial of shit is kitsch. I think he is only partly right. The denial of shit also invokes shit — that is exactly what I think of whenever the word indisposed floats into my purview. If, in some obscure Trollopean nineteenth-century novel, anyone is indisposed to do anything, there might as well be a graphically drawn commode to follow, perhaps with the inevitable (at least three times a week, my shit memory tells me) small turd floating at the bottom.

I learned, or needed, to use *indisposed* to cover my less quotidian bathroom activities. But this association stuck. The bathroom is still the only place I find masturbation comfortable, both for the obviously easy hygiene of it, and because masturbation can be as mnemonically sentimental as looking at old photographs, or mourning the uncapturable smells and tastes of childhood. Perhaps shit and kitsch are more reconcilable than one might at first think.

My mother would turn back up the stairs at my response to her. And something about her silence in doing so convinced me that she knew exactly what I was doing, there with my heavy-bear body assbackward on the toilet seat.

This scene, this sequence, came to be repeated several times a week, sometimes with unerring predictability. It got to the point where I knew that nine minutes after securing my onanistic sanctuary: *David! David!* thump, thump. I would vary times; I even tried a fake-out once or twice, going into the bathroom with no intention of doing anything. Nothing. So: I must confess that clearly I shared a mind-melded, masturbation-projection-prognostication relationship with my mother.

When my brother started taunting me with his discovery of my theft, it became all too clear what dastardly spilling-of-the-seed purpose it was being used for. Nothing was ever said directly until I couldn't take the tension any longer and spilled . . . the beans. It was a Sunday, and my brother had said something provocatively witty at the table, something along the lines of "hand lotion." My mother, at the kitchen sink, turned away. My father, in the *Sunday Times*, groaned or grunted with displeasure, rustled the paper annoyedly, and read on. My brother, as I recall the moment, was beaming with satisfaction at making me so unutterably uncomfortable. So much so, in fact, that I uttered; more than uttered, I outbursted. "All right already, I took it! I took the stupid hand lotion. And I masturbate. What am I supposed to do? I'm fourteen years old. What's the big deal?" I had the distinction of feeling simultaneously enlightened and repressed.

I had been reading *Portnoy's Complaint*, and I apparently did not yet understand that cultural confirmation of one's darkest suspicions, about self, about family, about even monkeys and masturbation, was no reason to bring this to anyone's attention, especially not the attention of what felt like my cultural oppressors and provocateurs themselves. In any case, my father lowered the paper, as though in slow motion, which should not come as any surprise since there is no way to lower a newspaper without it appearing in slow motion. He said (and now denies having said, but you know how that goes, he *really* did say it) that when he was my age he had the "real thing." I assumed he was not referring to Henry James. Even now, thinking of my father and Henry James locked in a sumptuous embrace, neither exactly thinking nor not thinking of that which was almost upon them, hanging fire, considering that either, in his deeper consciousness was no where closer . . . well, you get the point. My father uttered a classic cliché, one that you've heard somewhere, but never think you'll actually hear again. And, in all, or most, seriousness, I was both exasperated and grateful for it. Clichés are reassuring, after all; you know — at least I felt so at this moment — that you are sharing a cultural experience that has been oft repeated, time-tested, frequently wrongheadedly so. And the absurdity of his statement, his comparison, was a welcome distraction from the queasy sense of self present during those "hot" family boilerplate arguments, those times when you're sure you're in the right, and feel that you would rather be anywhere else, in stocks, or on a rack, than in the middle of a moment you know will leave you anything but vindicated.

My body lies over the sea . . .

Where would I have previously heard my father's shocking verity? I can't say, for certain. I'm sure the movies have a tamer version: *At your age I was working six days a week!* Or I had done this, seen that, been there, known such. The tenor was worldliness. In my mind: *whatever.* One thing my postwar generation (which I sometimes think of as postward, barely past, if at all, the familial enclave and our various psychological, or less charitably, psychodramatic, inheritances) has never adequately come to process is that while we are mostly more sophisticated than our parents in some ways — intellectually, technologically — and have had, perhaps, a veneer of experiences the previous middle class never had (trips to Europe and the like), we are not and will never be as worldly in the simple sense of accepting the fact that we must accommodate our choices, adjust our domains (domestic, local, national), and fit our selves into history, rather than trying to have history conform to us. But writing autobiographically is like looking through a double mirror at a room in which you continue to live in the past, a perpetual past life you believe you can change and which will then change you. The sin of self-serving interpretations looms like an automat over the entire process. This is why, after this essay, I will never write autobiographically again. I will write *noli me tangere* on my memory and drop the key to memory's safe-deposit box into the Hudson River, or any suitably dramatic body of water. Unless I come up with a good reason not to. Even Houdini usually had an escape clause, until his body couldn't find a way out.

Bring back, bring back, bring back my body . . .

Portnoy's Complaint did not introduce me to self-hatred and a distinct queasiness toward my claustrophobic (spatially and emotionally) family. I had hated my body, my distended stomach, and large appetite, fed by secretive trips to the fridge, for years. It merely affirmed it. I remember once exploding to my family; and as sick of self and family as I felt at the time, there is no way to render this without a touch of the comical: "We're just like the family Phillip Roth describes! Dad's constipated, in the bathroom for hours, and here I am . . . ," never daring to complete the sentence that would tell them about my trips to Manhattan prostitutes, fed by cash lifted from Mom's purse (an oedipal journey in itself, but those twenty-dollar bills seemed to have metastasized as my father's business took off; there were always a score of them in her inner purse compartment), never daring to reveal that I was so self-disgusted that masturbation became a way out of the body, out of the self, out of the row house, out of the family, out of the past endlessly rocking into distraction. It wasn't out of Brooklyn that I went, really. The body of Brooklyn, which is what I was, what I carted around, always came with me — that was why the fury of denial was always self-stoked. The more I tried to forget my body, the more self-disgust I acquired: I was a fat little perverted thief. And my family had even less of an idea of what *Portnoy's Complaint* was about than they had about the whirlpool that was going on inside my head.

It seemed like I was always retreating downstairs to my room, underground, as it were, and perhaps, in some sense, I remained there, brooding, feeling I was unmoved, listening to music from a strange assortment of song-fellows: The Who, Phil Ochs, Woody Guthrie, Joni Mitchell, the Carpenters, Grand Funk Railroad . . . until I went to college.

The second complication of my *Playboy*s was what disturbed and still disturbs me most, however (Let's say the train over the East River has stopped for a minute or two. We'll resume with it, I guarantee). I started noticing some of my magazines missing. I had many, but I had my favorites; my own inventory was right on the money. In a brazen move, I asked my mother if she had seen anything from my room upstairs. "Any what?" "Well, any books or magazines," I responded. "Uh-uh." Something in her voice caught. I was on the right track, a strange feat of intuition or deduction.

When my mother left the house I undertook a delicate search of her dresser drawers, a sometime favorite guilty pleasure by any means, raised to a distorted holy quest should my suspicions be vindicated. Which is the pleasure, of course, of rifling through someone else's belongings. It is, at the core, a quest for some kind of "real" story, literally the inside story. Once, years ago, I went through my girlfriend's correspondence looking for evidence of betrayal. I would have been satisfied with any kind of malfeasance. There was none. Of course, that in itself was final proof. I was enraged.

But this mission turned up its sexual grail. Beneath some linen and the smell of Ivory soap, two of my *Playboys* nestled. I returned them to their proper owner and prepared to await the consequences or watch for signs of change.

A slight edginess came and went. That was that. Thinking back, I can't remember speculating about why my mother took these magazines, incredible as that seems. But the game continued. I noticed some others gone. I asked again. "No, I haven't touched anything in your room." Then the retrieval, the justified drawer investigations, closet combing, careful to leave no tracks: Did the umbrella go in front of the shoes or behind them? Was that scarf on the floor? The smell of soap. Point counterpoint in an oedipal pas de deux. I accumulated magazines by the dozens, turning my room into a messy den of iniquity. And the command to "clean up your room" was never the same.

I'm still in the dark about my mother and the magazines. However, shortly before she died, I found in the living room table (yes, *in*; the table was hollowed out, a hiding place I never caught on to) one of the magazines with twenty or thirty pictures of women cut out of others. They were mostly of small, dark women. My mother was, indeed, small and dark. I've considered possibilities: curiosity, latency, jealousy . . . none seems more probable than the others. The rhetoric of who my mother was doesn't admit the incident readily: warm, self-sacrificing. Some of my understanding of her is less resistant: self-denying, deceptively smothering in a rather sweet way. I told the story to my brother after my mother's death: he was shocked, has never mentioned it again. It was a plea for understanding for complicated relationships, my keeping my distance from my mother. It was also revenge for my complete assumption of guilt about it all, the last revenge I remember consciously having taken.

My father's imprecation, my sense of my familial reputation, made me so paranoid, so confused about what I should be doing, that I convinced a friend to get a train and accompany me to a Manhattan massage parlor. The train moved. Hands across the water, indeed. We took our transistor radios and headed for Manhattan. On the way to the subway we heard Paul McCartney sing "hands across the water." I remember standing at the rear window of the train and watching two sides of Brooklyn, split by the tracks, pulling away from me. It was only in the distance, or past a curve, that the tracks vanished and Brooklyn was whole. I wasn't, by any means. I always tried to pick out the point on the bridge where one left the boundary of Brooklyn for that of Manhattan. The tunnels actually tell you: it was always strange to consider, no matter how dimly, that the only place where I could straddle these two territories, both with compelling, even competing, claims to my attention and affection, was underwater. And the line so clearly marked in the Brooklyn Battery Tunnel: ENTERING BROOKLYN. There should have been some kind of demilitarized zone between the two, where I could have stopped the car at times of little traffic and courted some refuge from the conflict, or cornered some disaffected tunnel cop who knew what that in-between world was like. We would drive through the tunnel, radio humming Nat King Cole or Tony Bennett, calm and yearning songs of yet another world. A sense of transgression invaded my sense of passing from Brooklyn to Manhattan that is still urgent, if mostly under control.

The massage parlor, our destination, was in an old building at 52nd Street and Broadway, an old office building, whose halls were used as models for B movies, halls where Sam Spade might have his office, or some pitifully unsuccessful theatrical agent. The office doors had the kind of thick, opaque glass that you don't see anymore, with names hand-lettered in rich black: ABRAHAM LERNER AND SONS, IMPORTERS, or SUGARMAN AND SUGARMAN, NOVELTIES AND SUNDRIES. One always had the impression that the original names were dead. I don't remember what was on the door of our destination, or the surrounding doors, some mercantile remnants, or just blank, the absence of name and number telling much, if not all.

We entered the shabby one-room office, split in two by a flimsy divider, repeated some time-honored false reassurances: "We're both eighteen. . . . We've been to places like this before. . . . We have girlfriends. . . . We work at Waldbaum's, Woolworth's, Walgreen's, Wal-Mart . . ."

I went first. The room was bare: a massage table, a chair, a sink (*a stone, a leaf, a door*, a sad motif that would repeat for years). My friend-for-hire was named Helen; she was Portuguese, and she launched me memorably. She turned my radio on: Bill Withers, "Lean on Me." She started massaging my back. I sat up and reached for my pants, handed her ten more dollars. She laughed. What did I want? I want you to touch me. Laughter. Where? Here. I also want to touch you. Where? Here (bosom covered by a gray sweater) and here (thigh covered with black stockings). Too shy to suggest anymore, to try and buy anymore, we proceeded. I wanted to kiss her. She pecked me occasionally on the lips, stiffly, as though we were two birds getting acquainted, or both shy youngsters. I was sitting on the edge of the table, she standing. She kept rocking her thighs on my knee, and I was by no means clear as to why. She got me off rather quickly, I dressed, and we went into the "waiting" room to give my friend his turn. I discovered, to my dismay, as we sat and waited, that I was in love with Helen. I kept asking to kiss her, and she seemed delighted by my idiocy in a rather maternal way. I couldn't bear the idea of stopping the kisses. Unfortunately, her boss came in, a tall black man who scared the hell out of me on the basis of those two facts in that context — talk about cultural inheritance. He was very agitated about my obviously deficient age. Soon after we trudged out, down, toward home, hands across the water, for my still-hungry and uncertain first nonvirginal trip across the river, not thinking of the river and bridge's dividing line, nor the architecture of my first sexual experience. All I kept thinking was "What have I done, and how can I do it again."

Also at fourteen, I went to see a prostitute at Dante's Inferno, a hair salon on West Fifty-sixth Street that was a front for a massage parlor, and she told me to not gain any more weight. She had let me rub my penis on her stomach before she slicked her hand to give me my release. I got off the D train at West Fourth Street and called her from a pay phone to tell her I loved her: "I think you're a beautiful person both physically and emotionally." I actually said stuff like that when I was fourteen. She said I was sweet and maybe if I came again I could bring another ten dollars and she'd do something very special for me, and really, don't put any more weight on.

Small and dark. My mother used to listen to music all the time. She would buzz around the kitchen singing popular songs—"The Very Thought of You," "I Get a Kick Out of You"—and show tunes—"Hello, Young Lovers," "There's a Boat That's Leaving for New York." I thought that there was no mystery in these. And when she told me she liked to listen to songs because they made her cry, I was disdainful. I walked out of the room shaking my head in tolerant mockery, only to find myself, years later. singing them to myself, giving little concerts to friends, and trying to remember what the circumstances of my first exposures were to the body of work that had surrounded me.

I pulled away, began the years of my secret life, aspects of which still linger. I especially needed, clearly, to get some distance from the oedipal drama — stoked by chopped liver, salami sandwiches, potato pancakes, stuffed cabbage — that I was doing a fat-boy dance version of with my mother. My narrative is as fragmented here as my sense of my body has been. Does this qualify as imitative form?

I started making my own meals, which might not sound like much, but resonated sorrowfully in defining my relationship with my mother for the thin few years remaining until she was to waste away, from smoking the cigarettes that have helped keep me thin for almost twenty years. I've heard all the smoking arguments, the smoking guns, as it were, and witnessed my own mother's death. My father, in response to my smoking, varies in his jeremiads to me; *you've seen what it can do* can become *she never inhaled*, based on a moment's psychological necessity. I understand that necessity with an ease that belies my own inability to trade in "my old addiction," as Chet Baker so lamentably and lovingly refers to his own dependency so close to the end, for a longer and potentially heavier life. The idea that dying earlier than is at all necessary is less powerful than the fear of fathood should give you, does give me, some idea of the hold, the continuing grip of my need to see myself as, if not thin (something I have never been able to pull off psychologically, no matter what my weight), at least not fat. I do think about the smoking; I have nights of terror when I dream a giant cloud composed of twenty years of exhalations comes and sweeps me into a vaporous smoke ghost. Smoke is, after all, the ghost of ash.

And what looks better with a cigarette than a black T-shirt and black jeans? Several of my colleagues, in expressing their high wit and subtle perceptiveness, have a habit of asking me about my habit of wearing black: "What, no black today?" they'll ask with a charming brio, a couture-aware élan. In truth, I do wear much black; in fact, I also frequently wear other, mostly subdued colors. But my history of blackness, my noirishness, did not originate with beatness, hipness, coolness, or a photo of Jean-Paul Belmondo or James Dean. Black began with Shirley, a friend of mother's, telling me, circa 1970, that I looked good in black, *it's so slimming.* A little light went off, a black one, that has stayed lit for all these years. I'm always on the lookout for the perfect black shirt, despite the fifteen or so that already line my burgeoning closets. I once dreamt that I was walking on a familiar street, one of those combinations of here and there, then and now, Brooklyn and some other place, all twisted into something so recognizable that, in the dream, despite your relative contentment, you feel that something has to be wrong, although what that might be is lost in the daze of a narrative that you're dimly aware is unfolding from some point out there, coming toward you like a backward string of dominoes. I was walking along, walking in the pavement, on the sun, when I realized I was wearing a shirt with horizontal stripes, a wardrobe feature I have avoided like the nonblack plague. I was horrified. I knew, instinctively, that the horizontal stripes were making me look chubby, and I seemed to bloat out as I walked. The cold sweat I woke with, the trembling fear, was the equal of any apocalyptic, behemoth-filled nightmare I had ever had. I think I had a sense that there would be no end to my expanding body, no boundaries or borders; that I would expand until I covered the borough of Brooklyn and elsewhere. I do know that the next day I wore black jeans and a stylish, black, Italian silk shirt, buttoning and unbuttoning the top button all day, not quite sure which looked best, but knowing that a man in black, the bohemian minister, was almost always hiding something, and hiding it well.

As a Lazar, as a nominal son of Lazarus, am I not entitled to more than one life, to have the body's determination reversed? In an ancient and archaic definition, Lazar means black. Should I not honor my etymology as well as my genealogy? Then again: "Dives," he said, "for God's sake watch what yr doing." And Lazar is a synonym for leper, an unclean person, a degraded body. But what's in a name, after the name is laid bare. Does a name's narrative become threadbare? Or does it bare the thread: black?

I am in good company, though. Anytime one can quote Charles Lamb, even if a bit of a stretch, should be counted as a prodigious blessing, an opportunity contentful and consanguine, be it in his mirth or his cups, his doleful rue or most easily rendered and lightly worn sagacity.

To be able to cite Lamb on both cigarettes and the wearing of black, the former from "Confessions of a Drunkard," the latter from "The Wedding," is nothing short of a kind of *coup d'essai*, a blessing of the Lamb.

Black has been my ordinary apparel so long — indeed I take it to be the proper costume of an author — the stage sanctions it. . . . I should repel my readers, from a mere incapacity of believing me, were I to tell them what tobacco has been to me, the drudging service which I have vowed to it. How, when I have resolved to quit it, a feeling as of ingratitude has started up; how it has put on personal claims and made the demands of a friend upon me. . . . How, even now, when the whole secret stands confessed in all its dreadful truth before me, I feel myself linked to it beyond the power of revocation. Bone of my bone —

Flesh of my flesh. Black as an almost alternate flesh, black as my lungs are no doubt getting, smoke the ghostly extension of flesh. My bones carry a lighter weight now, have for quite some while, having left so much excess flesh in Brooklyn, for Brooklyn to carry, in memory, all of my excess weight. This author, properly or not, is costumed in black, paying for his sometimes dyspeptic — the thick cough, the stale, lifeless smell of clothes, rooms, some memories — sometimes sweet consortment with cigarettes. Charles, if I may so call you (thou?), to borrow you one more time: "I have no puling apology to make for mankind" ("Confessions"). This is not a confession, after all, in the sense of the confessional. Rather, as I believe here, as is so in everything autobiographical I write, the motive is to try and understand why I am so absurd, and hopefully to undertake this journey entertainingly, engagingly, so that my hypocrite lecteur can feel that she and he are absurd, too. In this way, a kind of secret society of neurotics, compulsives, obsessive self-examiners, can form a kind of literary fraternity, and go about our messy business a bit more comfortably without necessarily having to change anything. I am neither trying to be arch, nor glib, despite how amusingly either can on occasion be performed. I just want to make sure that you understand that my model as an essayist, a memoirist, is anything but heroic, unless one's conception of heroism is leavened with, expanded by, a sense of the absurd. Give me Hazlitt's *Liber Amoris*, that much reviled, then forgotten, piece of nineteenth-century experimentation (memoir as novel of transparently autobiographical revelation in which the narrator is completely self-aware and yet reaches no staggering epiphanies, issues no proclamations declaring a reformed self). You see, and I won't tell if you won't, this is an essay.

What does it mean when we are complimented on our clothes? Is there a difference between "You look good" and "That's a great-looking shirt"? Clearly there is, as we know from the slightly queasy feeling we get saying thank you when an item of clothing is praised, as though we partook in its qualities, its aura. In either case, though, I take compliments as acknowledgment of my sense of taste, rather than as an affirmation of the way I look. The latter, at times, seems unimaginable to me, the best that can be hoped for a rather smart packaging of rather ordinary stuff. I must admit, or at least I will, that I haven't considered the former ordinary for quite some time. It started sometime around the age of thirteen, when I became aware that I was always aware of my body and always watching, that in almost every given social situation I was probably seeing more, which is to say seeing a greater variety of angles, perspectives, aware, always aware, of what others were saying, what I was saying, what everyone was wearing, how they were moving, how they were standing still, how their eyes darted or lingered, how words were pronounced and articulated, the almost imperceptible reactions to speech and movement, the almost imperceptible implications of words, of bodies. This is not an unusual development for outsiders. And it was, it still is, a blessing and a curse: difference, otherness. There is a wonderful moment in the film *Broadcast News* when Holly Hunter's honcho network boss, in reaction to her complete self-assurance, says that it must be wonderful to know that you're always the smartest person in a room. Hunter, completely sincerely, brow furrowed, replies, "No, it's horrible." I certainly don't always feel that I'm the smartest person in a room, but I usually feel that I'm the person in a room who is most considering the social situation and implications of every action, every reaction. The person choosing his words most carefully, though not always cautiously. I am frequently also the man with the nicest clothes. I would like to say that none of this is accompanied by the presumption that I feel elevated by these feelings, but old defenses die slowly, if at all. Call me Jerico. The sense that I was seeing everything going on was akin to feeling that I was the omniscient narrator who controlled nothing. All sensibility, no control. No wonder I fell for Henry James. No wonder the intellectual and aesthetic confidence I began projecting in my twenties, accompanied by social discomfort and uncertainty, was attractive to smart women who had grown tired of traditional masculine fortitude. My retiring, neurotic, dryly witty persona fit the age. Mon dieu! (Mon diable!); I was in vogue, the feminized man, with all the stereotypical qualities that have made gay men attractive to women as friends: overdeveloped body consciousness, willingness to talk about feelings, apparent vulnerability, and a love for shopping, especially for clothes. Two hitches: I much preferred Frank Sinatra to Judy Garland, and I wanted to go to bed with just about every attractive woman I met.

Making the Man:
A brief consideration of my wardrobe

I have more clothes than anyone I know. My wardrobe includes twenty-two sport jackets, four suits, four winter coats (including a black wool car coat, collar trimmed with black suede, bought at Harrod's post-Christmas sale in 1986; a leather parka; and a leather, belted, heavy jacket-length coat), approximately ninety shirts (including thirty or forty "retro" shirts from the fifties), fourteen pairs of pants (although I wear black jeans seventy-five percent of the time), fifteen pairs of shoes, seventeen light jackets (one leather, one suede), ten vests, three fedoras (black, green, gray), fifty or so T-shirts, and assorted sweaters (not my favorite garment — almost never slimming) and other accoutrements. My favorite outfit is relatively simple: black jeans, black T-shirt, smart sport jacket, sharp pair of shoes. But I also like an occasional foray into something more dandyish, say a black velvet vest with Nehru collar, white linen collarless shirt underneath, black silk pants, Italian-blend three-button sport coat in a rich, muted blue check, bottomed out by Kenneth Cole black slip-ons with a silver bar on the instep. Frequently I'll simply wear a retro shirt with black jeans. Since descriptions of clothes are singularly uninteresting, I'll stop here, and say this: I used to go shopping with my mother, just the two of us, small peregrinations into Manhattan to the old Barney's, when it was a large store with excellent discounted selections. We'd have lunch at a diner, or small inexpensive restaurant, usually catch a movie. Even though I was only eleven or twelve, there was no thought to censoring what I could see. We caught *A Clockwork Orange* one summer matinee; I thought it terribly clever. Invariably, on these outings, some item, a jacket, a shirt, would catch my eye, slightly more expensive than the kind of thing we were wont to buy, something a bit on the dear side. After some hesitation that I would know was going to fold, she bought it for me. I would think it lovely, would look forward to taking it home, trying it on for her. She would ooh and aahh and take great pleasure in both her ability to buy me what I wanted and my evident interest in self-adornment. And there was always, after this, a moment of stunning disappointment when I went back downstairs, posed in front of my grandparents' ominously large Deco mirror, and realized that I was a bloated body wearing a pleasing but large covering, that no item, no selection, no understanding of color or cut, of fashion, of garments, could make me more than a moderately well-dressed freak. Today, with more pleasing if innocuous shapes, I'm still always trying to experience that moment when looking good is as much a prerogative of my body as of my clothes.

My closest friend from about age nine to twelve was a boy named Billy Meylach. He was very slight, with dark curly hair, an olive complexion, buck teeth, and an admirable singing voice. I still remember that even those toughs and cool guys admitted that he sang "I Won't Grow Up," from *Peter Pan*, with, if I can recall the exact Brooklyn diction, "a kind of sangfroid for the mot juste that did the song eminent justice." Words to that effect; they liked it, and probably stopped tormenting him as the school faggot for fifteen minutes or so. As someone with no cache, Billy was a rather poor choice for me socially. I was usually the next-to-last person chosen for sports, Billy the last. Whereas my sluggish frame performed poorly (which would stunningly change after I lost my weight, freed of baggage both physical and psychological), I at least had the forms down. My throws were regulation boy-throws, my swinging the bat inept, but, well, in the ball game. Billy was one of those boys who have a very pure kind of effeminacy. To invoke the lexicon of a less-enlightened time, he looked like a girl doing just about everything, including standing still. We did everything together, short of anything sexual, though I'm sure we had terrible crushes on each other for a good two years. And as so suddenly would happen to me later in life, I abruptly fell out of love with him at some point, and became quite cruel for a while. I seem to remember that this had a devastating effect on him, the crush crushed. But I think, emerging from a kind of confusing latency, I needed friends who were at least plausible as boys, as males, as boy-men. My own version of the feminine worked more quietly: I noticed clothing, everyone's clothing. I was modest to the point of primness about exposing my body (Here I will spare the reader a spate of locker-room stories that have been too well captured in literature and on film to bear repetition). I spoke quietly, cried easily. And as my adolescence shaded into my teens, I developed the watchfulness that clever outsiders usually develop, needing as we do to be more aware of the codes and the possible consequences of breaching social boundaries, standards, expectations.

I give you, for example, the case of Debbie Whalen. She was a classmate in junior high, David A. Boody Junior High, to be exact. My three years there, between 1968 and 1971, were nothing short of my mortification, the psychological and physical debasement that led to my resurrection as a thin man. Debbie Whalen didn't abuse me, except by her complete unreachability to someone as physically unattractive as I was. She wore black skirts with slits, black stockings, and black pumps about twice a week, but always, for some reason, on Thursday. She was tall, with long, straight, dirty-blonde hair and a face that looked like a cross between an Irish milkmaid's — clear complected, pale — and a Modigliani; it elongated near the chin. I looked at her ankles constantly and made much pleasant conversation with her. She was always very nice. Very nice indeed. In the way that told you that she was being nice because she was very nice, and that you really didn't exist at all except as a presence that crossed her path regularly and therefore engaged her niceness. I could have crawled right out of *The Metamorphosis*, apple sticking out of my back as I scurried in front of her, and Debbie would have been really . . . nice. What was infuriating was that she had a touch of the bad girl in her seductiveness and obliviousness, and so one couldn't even really begrudge her niceness. Even as she was acting terribly nice, I knew that she thought half the time that I didn't exist and she was conversing with a kind of nice spectre, and half the time was proving her niceness by a slight physical distaste, deftly almost-hidden, that, nice as she was, she tried to conceal and I had no trouble detecting. My antennae, you see, were entirely flexible, subtle, and sensitive. I must have found this slight, really almost undetectable aversion stimulating in some way. Not only could I have written epics about her ankles, which fascinated me — so slender — but she was my major erotic obsession for at least two years. No bout of self-satisfaction in that time ever neglected her for at least a passing scenario. Frequently I began with her, her unapproachable and slightly stupid allure just getting me going when the inevitable and unexpected maternal interruption would let the air right out of her allure. Perhaps my mother could read my mind only sexually, and specifically disapproved of Debbie Whalen. I was separated from my leben love by more than mere tonnage, though. If I had been a princely, affable sort of Jewish boy, I might have been able to make some time, though this sort of crossover between Jewish and Catholic was frowned upon (not so among the same sex). But to be Jewish, fat, somewhat shy, and fond of occasional enigmatic ripostes would not do at all. She signed my yearbook "To a nice guy," not knowing I had been defiling her gleefully for years. I had given up devoted Billy for unapproachable Debbie. To this day, I think about my own level of effeminacy, always think some quality in me — the way I move, or the way I stand still — falls short of the manly. And the women in my life have mostly been very nice, very non-Jewish, and very willing to accept my insinuations in lieu of sexual aggression and to make the crucial first moves.

But David A. Boody Junior High School provided another event, which led to a long series of events that more than anything else defined my sense of self as body-betrayed, a creature outside the realm of normal bodies; a thing apart, and therefore distinct, and therefore superior, and utterly miserable. Eddy Moore threw a firecracker at me. We were sitting in assembly, seventh grade, and Billy Meylach was sitting between us. The Moore Boys, as they were known, were Mafia kids. At least that was the word on them. Why Mafia kids would be named Moore was an anomaly that was acknowledged as unresolvable. They were the toughest of the tough kids, the kinds who drew blood in fights. In *The Wanderers*, Richard Price's wonderfully surreal meditation on gangs and sex in the early sixties, one of the gangs, the Wongs, appears and says, "Nobody fucks with the Wongs." Nobody fucked with the Moores. It was decided, as though by plebiscite, that they were too powerful and too weird for anyone else to take on. Plus, when you took one Moore on, you took them all. If getting slaughtered by one Moore was unthinkable, getting slaughtered by all of them was exponentially unthinkable. That is what we thought.

The firecracker wasn't lit. I jumped, and Eddy Moore laughed a sick little laugh. All of the Moores were slightly defective in the head. Eddy didn't bother with Billy because he was in permanent torment, and therefore untormentable. Not enough fun there. I was merely in perpetual torment; if I ventured out of my subgroup of reasonably smart Italian and Jewish kids, in the special programs, I was liable to be punched at any time. Simply for being fat and looking like I was concerned that at any moment I might be punched. Being fat was a great inducement to punching. Everyone knew that fat kids didn't fight well, or at all — that they were pampered, soft, feminine. Plus, there is the target factor, and what I imagine was a certain amount of pleasure at a fist connecting with a plump belly, rather like punching a pillow. I just went and punched a pillow and it felt very good, so I think my reasoning not completely untoward. There was an occasional slob who was kind of tough and would fight, wasn't in the sissy club, but generally the fat kids had had the idea that they couldn't fight ingrained for so long that a kind of flinching developed as their second nature. As a matter of fact, there was a kind of flinching game that developed and lasted for a year or two at Boody. You would go up to someone and feign a punch, and if the punchee flinched, you got to hit him three times in the arm. Strangely, though, you had to follow this by "wiping it off," and if you failed to do so the punchee became the puncher and was given three free shots. This, too, had to be wiped off, and so on. Naturally, some kids were more frequent flinching targets than others. Other than with a few friends, no one had too much worry about playing the flinch game with me. I certainly didn't want to give an excuse to anyone to murderize me, which is what would have happened if I had made a tough kid flinch. I would have gotten my three free punches, and then had the living daylights knocked out of me. I believe this defines pyrrhic victory.

I digress. I jumped, Eddy Moore started laughing, then having finished laughing, stopped and told me to hand the firecracker over. In Brooklynese this was probably something like, "Awright, hand id back ovah heah." Despite formidable odds and the usual unthinkable, I declined. I actually reasoned with him, as though such a thing were possible. "Eddy," I said, "it's one thing to throw the firecracker at me, but asking me to pick it up and give it back is unreasonable." Several moments later, when I managed to remove the crook of his arm from my neck, I went speeding out of the auditorium, into the first-floor hall, in bloody terror.

Straight into the arms of Mr. Caliendo, the assistant principal. Asked what I was doing in the hall, I confessed immediately. Perhaps this moment was the beginning of what would become a well-developed sense of duplicity. This moment, with its disastrous consequences, added to, the following year, the beginning of my secret teenage excursions with whores, left me with the desire, ability, and urge to keep some central part of my life to myself, to always have some central part of my life that was unshareable, that was to last . . . let's say for a very long time.

Writing a story one has repeated and refined over the years can be a frustrating experience. Is there enough discovery for me here, other than the odd felicities of voice, the verbal connections, the jokes? When is written autobiographical narrative as vibrant as oral narrative? When it is endless, when the subject as object is larger than the subject as subject? When repetition transcends compulsion? Maybe what has created certain twentieth-century lifelong autobiographers like Michel Leiris is a sense of the epic married to the absurd.

I do.

I confessed, and Moore was called into the principal's office. For the next several months, every day, without fail, at lunch in the cafeteria, a group of Moores and hangers-on would pick me up, place me against the wall, form a semicircle around me, and tell me, graphically, how they were going to destroy me, knock the fat flesh out of me, flay me, fuck me, and leave me for dead. I was petrified, even though my flesh jiggled and I had rather supple breasts. I wanted to go home, but at home they were very concerned and very removed from my trauma. There must be some way, there must be some place, there must be someone who understood that life was not right. That being pushed and bullied (one of the charmers would come, like clockwork, every day at 12:10, squeeze my sandwich, and take a big bite out of it), that being terrorized was not the way it was supposed to be. But that was the way it was, not the week that was, but the year and a half that was.

You would think they would have gotten bored with the ritual, or I would have been sedated by it. After all, I wasn't sodomized or pulverized. Yet the Moore capacity for vengeance, the baby Sicilian need to exterminate me, and my own receptivity to fear and self-loathing (Why didn't I just hand the fucking firecracker back?) were seemingly unlimited.

At one point, I was so miserable that my mother requested a meeting with the principal, an entirely impotent man named Meyer Whitlin. The Jewish kids, normally respectful, called him Witless. Nobody else knew exactly who he was. My mother and I, with Eddy Moore and his mother, gathered in Witless's office. He undoubtedly said something, the verbal equivalent of tapioca pudding. I only remember Eddy's mother striding toward me, threatening, saying, "He's such a fat boy, can't he take care of himself? He's not big enough to fight?" I thought *she* was going to fight me. Didn't happen.

The terror continued. Louis Klieger, the son of a judge, a smart kid who found life with tougher kids more interesting, or rewarding, or psychologically necessary, told me, half with sympathy, half with relish, that half the school was talking about killing me. Thanks, Louie. I bet you're a judge now, too.

During this time, I was resisting going to school so much, seemed so depressed, that my family doctor prescribed some pills, vitamins he said. A few days later I felt much better. My daily tribulations almost seemed amusing at times. The pills ran out and I gradually slipped back into despair. And then, a year and a half or so after the initial debacle, in the middle of eighth grade, having settled into a kind of pathological acceptance of terror, the whole thing broke in rather storybook fashion. Singing saved me, much as it had temporarily halted the ritual abuse of my first love, Billy.

A guy named Vinny sat next to me in vocal music class. I don't remember how well I sang, but I know I was regarded as the best in the class, the belle of the ball, if only for my performance on the exams we were given, whose nature escapes me entirely. Vinny was a tough guy. I knew him by reputation. He wasn't very smart, but we sat together, and for some reason he was always very nice to me. Very, there is no other way to say it, solicitous. Because of this unexpected gentleness from an unexpected quarter, I gladly let him cheat off of me on exams.

He did this well, and imperfectly, which in cheating works out perfectly, and was entirely grateful.

One day, Vinny said to me, in true Corleone fashion, "I understand you have a problem." I believe I said, in response, "Yes, Vinny, I have a problem." Vinny, a rather understated kid verbally, though he had rather active and intelligent eyes, said significantly, "Okay. Let's see about that." The next vocal music class period ended, and we all headed toward the door to the school yard for recess, otherwise known by me as the Land of Horrors. At the door stood Eddy Moore, one of his accomplices, Moore or un-Moored, beside him. He beaded a look at me as we approached, Vinny and I. Vinny gestured me aside, firmly but with the air of a gentleman who knew his class, his privilege. He walked up to Eddy and eyeballed him from about two centimeters. All he said was, "What's the problem?" and stood there. The unthinkable happened. Eddy blinked. A Moore blinked. Vinny gave me a princely gesture, telling me to go through, go out, leave the auditorium. I squeezed by and walked into a desultory spring sun, but sun nonetheless. And no one, no Moore, no Body, ever systematically threatened me again. A principle was established: I was fat, I was unmasculine, but I was not necessarily outside the world of a certain kind of power. I could write, I could share what I had written, what I knew, and a sleek barbaric jerk would back down, while a sleek barbaric sweetheart took me under the wing. This, too, was good company, though I believe my friendship with Vinny wilted without the pressure of either his failing grade or the assurances, on any given day, of my assured destruction. This was, after all, no sentimental bonding of unlike kinds, but a beautiful temporary alliance built on sincere respect for complementary deficiencies. I seem to remember that we nodded toward each other in the halls, and on rare occasions exchanged muted, conspiratorial half-smiles.

The sixties and early seventies were the Age of the Sitcom and the high-fat commercial break. Commercial breaks, after all, were universally acknowledged as snack breaks, bubbles of time to prepare food to accompany Rob and Laura, Mary and Lou and Ted and Murray, Bob and Howard and Carol, Archie and Edith, Lucy and anybody. I would make open-faced salami sandwiches (think slices of Hebrew National on rye), bowls full of Breyer's Cherry Vanilla, which I liked to eat with pretzels, six or seven Oreos and milk for dunking. And there is that postcoital moment after a snack when you want a little more, when you realize you had been watching the show and not paid attention to the last few bites. To do the snack justice, another two slices of salami, another two Oreos to dunk in the black-speckled remainder of milk. I ate my way through more commercials than Nabisco or Kraft could possibly have paid for, and the joke was on them since I hardly saw a fraction of what they were trying to get me to want. I learned to go about this stealthily, since comments about my indulgence started in my adolescence around the same time as comments about my fatness. I would lightly open the refrigerator in the dark, still a decadent-living image I savor — light and temptation — and make sure no package wrapped in foil or plastic screamed out a warning. When my father caught me, he would look at me and the plate askance, slightly amused and slightly disgusted, and ask, "What's the matter, don't they feed you at home?" My mother would tell me to "enjoy." My brother would comment or not, depending on whether a truce existed, calling for relative diplomacy. If not, I would be addressed as one of the countless variations of fat names, from animals to famous fat persons. I still steal food. At parties, at friends' houses, I like to sneak food from the table or the refrigerator, like to take food unseen, that is, food that would be gladly given, and seen as a sign that I do, in fact, eat.

And then there is the matter of Stephen Lipshitz. What's in a name, indeed. If I was near the bottom rung, Lipshitz was nowhere near the ladder. He was the most otherwordly creature I have ever encountered, another classmate in junior high. I wrote a poem when I was in my early twenties that canonized him: St. Lipshitz, a martyr to the cause of what? Of the purest otherness. Of bodies and minds in torment? Lipshitz's parents must have been poor observant Jews; he wore a shoddy black suit, stained, oversized white shirt, black tie, every day. And carried that impossible large black valise. We continually wondered what could be in there, although part of us didn't want to know, thinking perhaps that Lipshitz, the maladjusted, less assimilated, crazy version of us would open it at some point and out would spill the magical sand of the Baal Shem, the revered Hasidic mystic, which would surround our feet, engulf us, drag us back from whence our people came, a thought utterly horrifying when you've grown up on a diet of the Mets and *Lost in Space*. Lipshitz had a perennial scowl on his face, short, dark, messy curls. He was progerialike, preternaturally middle-aged, thin and bent; no: hunched. He was even too weird for the tough kids to beat up. They would give him an occasional shove, as would the picked-on kids, delighted to have *somebody* they could threaten. This, Rube Goldberg–like, would induce the Lipshitz special: he would lift one leg and make a slow kicking motion, as though he were performing a pantomime. At the same time his scowl would deepen, he would swing his briefcase to clear the space around him, and, this was the capper, he would hiss.

Several years later, in college, I ran into an old junior high acquaintance I hadn't seen since, and the talk turned to Lipshitz. We were undoubtedly taking similar classes, because we said, almost simultaneously: Gregor Samsa. I had been terrorized, had been made to feel repulsive, but at least I occupied a place in the human camp. Lipshitz haunted us with his physical and psychic distance from anything remotely familiar. He was our rickety, forgotten, cultural history embodied, a nightmare.

As the novelty of junior high waxed into waning and then waned into waxing, the specter of a more mature life as a fatso, an asexual, unathletic, oedipally beleaguered, thieving whoremonger began to perturb me. One Sunday afternoon in my fourteenth year, I decided to go on a diet. I remember that it was spring, because the day was light, light and mild, the kind of day that wears its light lightly. I did not want high school to commence the next September with an image of me in my fat glory for all to savor. I wanted to have a life replete with normal rejections from girls. As it was, I was never rejected, because the idea of approaching a girl — and as with, I imagine, many of the physically deficient, I was not at all interested in fat or unattractive girls — was completely out of the question. Debbie Whalen was merely the symbolic tip of a generally icy response to me from girls.

I announced to my family that I was going to lose "the weight." Not some weight, or my weight. This weight was almost another presence in the family. My father would sometimes say, "When are you going to lose the weight?" I would sometimes ask my mother about the possibility of going to a special camp to "do something about the weight." When my brother wanted to annoy me, he would play The Band's "The Weight." He was also partial to "He Ain't Heavy, He's My Brother."

I started to wear a black, rubber, corsety thing that wrapped around your middle and attached with Velcro. I had seen it on TV, demonstrated by someone like Buster Crabbe, who in my childhood and adolescence was identified as the star who was a star because he was so identified but couldn't be much of a star because he was always pitching humiliating and castrating products for aging male vanity, like the tight T-shirt that disguised your flab, or the rubber corset that made you sweat your pounds away. I started wearing the rubber at all times; I even slept with it on, and was perpetually sweating, perpetually dripping like a leaky condom.

I started running and shooting baskets as often as I could. And food became the desired enemy, the compulsion that needed to be resisted. It became the bookend of sex, the compulsion that couldn't be resisted. Once these had been properly identified, I developed a perfect system of rewards, allowing myself to indulge in the irresistible compulsion if I managed to resist the resistible compulsion, self-gifted with the extra round of masturbation, the especially nasty pornographic magazine, and of course the occasional visit to a prostitute. I still felt rather vile about the latter enterprise, notably the need to steal for it. But I felt I was engaged in the single pursuit that had the possibility of dramatically altering my life, and justifying its incentives was far from tortuous.

I started counting every calorie, cutting out anything fried, anything fatty, anything rich. I started cooking for myself. This created a disturbance that my family, with their laments for my good looks lost in a sea of flab, a supposedly handsome face bobbing in a blubbering ocean like a buoy, had not anticipated. My mother's food began to be rejected. Rhoda had her own deal with food and weight, I realized years later. She had been a fat kid, too (as had my babushka grandmother, Rose), and had lost her weight in her early teens, as well. My mother was always skipping meals or eating extraordinarily light ones. Thinking about her eating, all that comes to mind is coffee in a tall class, a Breakstone cottage cheese jar, actually. And a slice of challah with cottage cheese on top. Clearly this was theme eating. I simply cannot summon another image. She was always fussing about her weight, but that burden our culture feeds women with was and is not unusual. Nevertheless, I remember my father bringing home boxes and boxes of dresses for her to try on while he ate, a slightly obscene fashion show, as though he were eating off her body. (This rather vulgar interpretation brought to you by years of Freudian, Lacanian, Post-Freudian, and Post-Lacanian discourse. It shows a certain disgruntlement at the idea of food and sex innocently conjoined by my parents. But as these parents' child, I take the responsibility to refuse to dwell on such things, or to dismiss them interpretively. Consider it done; I've had my cake, eaten it, and can now be called essayistically bulimic.) As one might imagine, the shopping forays with my mother abruptly ceased.

Somebody, please, stop me before I digress again.

If the dresses didn't quite fit, I remember a mournful mother, a response on her part that surpassed annoyance, even self-disgust. Extremes, after all, can be more easily diagnosed and treated than some chronic and supposedly benign conditions. Her sadness seemed deep, but passed in a flash, retracted to a private place. I shiver when I think of how my brother and I would squeeze her upper arms and call her flabby arms. This was done innocently, I think, at least by my brother. I can't remember my own motives, other than a kind of sexual response, which made me refrain from the practice at the first quivering of this consciousness. She would laugh heartily, though with the same flicker of sadness riding behind her eyes.

My mother fed us all individually. We ate together only on the weekends. I'm not sure how this evolved. I know that my father frequently came home late from his office, too late for us kids to eat with him. But my mother ended up serving my brother and me at different times, bringing our food into the little TV room that had been our bedroom; we ate on TV tables, watching the four-thirty movie, Bette Davis or George Raft or one of those wonderful fifties sci-fi films like *The Angry Red Planet*, or *Dark Shadows*, or *Jeopardy* with Art Flemming (that erudite host of a former age — I have vowed to mention him in an essay in gratitude for an early example of convivial gentlemanliness). We were trained to be served. If we needed more soda, more food, more anything, we'd merely shout down the hall to the kitchen–dining room, where my mother would be reading at the table, and she would succor our request. To this day, I am uncomfortable being served by women; it feels creepy and fetishistic to have food placed in front of me. At family gatherings, when dinner is ready to be brought to the table, or dinner is done, my brother and I are always first to jump up and bring the dishes in, take the dishes out. I believe that while doing so we have expressions of penance, of unction, on our faces.

The foods we ate were New World–shtetl, a combination brocaded from Russian and other Eastern European ghettos and American television. This led to strange combinations and schizophrenic, alternating menus. Here is one possible week's menu:

Monday: chulaptchas (stuffed cabbage) and mashed potatoes
Tuesday: Swanson fried-chicken TV dinners
Wednesday: Kasha varnishkes and split-pea soup with marrow bones, the point being to suck or drag out the sweet little meat spot
Thursday: hamburgers with frozen french fries
Friday, which almost never varied: a small glass of tomato juice, homemade chopped liver with a sliced tomato, homemade chicken soup with a single large carrot in every bowl, roasted chicken with canned peas and carrots. We almost never celebrated the Sabbath other than by this ritual meal, served, of course, separately.
Saturday: We frequently ate out in Manhattan, before going to the theater. For years we went to Orsini's, on Fifty-sixth Street between Fifth and Sixth Avenues. Italian haute cuisine. We began our meals there with plates of scampi and fried mozzarella. The maitre d' there, Isadoro, when asked to make us something special, would wink and make us stewed veal and chopped vegetables, which we were always delighted by. Or we would go to a more family-style restaurant frequented by many in the travel industry, Nick and Guido's, on Forty-sixth Street's restaurant row, west of Eighth Avenue.
Sundays were the only day we had two meals together. For years we went to the Hong Kong restaurant in Brooklyn, near King's Plaza. We always arrived precisely at noon. I remember the owner's unlocking the door and allowing us to walk into that sweet-and-sour aroma in a dark room with booths. Later in my teens we switched to Sunday lunches brought home from the delicatessen: hot dogs with sauerkraut, a pound of sliced tongue and corned beef, enormous dill pickles, a mound of potato salad, which my brother and I wolfed down after Sunday-morning softball games at Marine Park

with guys named Piz and Stick and Kong. After feasting, I'd sleep much of the afternoon in the summer on a Naugahyde love seat in front of a Mets or Yankees baseball game. Sunday dinner was invariably "dairy," which then and now reminds me of trips to a world that, for all intents and purposes, no longer exists: New York's dairy restaurants. Their intents and purposes were rather clear: repositories of starch, keepers of the formulae of Eastern European shtetl cooking. Sunday night we would eat plates of tuna or mashed sardines or canned salmon, with slices of cucumber and onion, the latter accompanied by a little mound of salt for dipping. Raw onion is still one of my great delights. Maybe with a slice of pumpernickel smeared with butter. What, as we used to say, could be bad.

What was bad for me at the time was being fat, the prospect of which still controls every bite I take of every food I ever eat. So my multicultural meals, the United Nations of foods my mother served forth, with the United States and Russia the only permanent members of the security council, had to disband. The rub here is that cooking was, perhaps, my mother's primary mothering function. This is not to say she lacked other maternal resources; far from it. Rhoda was and remains the Ur-mother for me; not just my mother, but *the* mother. She succeeded, in some ways too well, at providing comfort, attention, encouragement. So much so that well into my junior high school debacles, I would feign illness to stay home from school with her, to spend the day with her, playing cards and Monopoly, Scrabble. But food was central, and all food she made was somehow comfort food. It was worth being sick to have her make latkes, or a big bowl of creamy mashed potatoes. Throw in some comic books, *Courageous Cat and Minute Mouse*, or *Diver Dan* or *Sky King* on morning TV, and who would want to ever go to school, leave the house, leave the kitchen? Once, in the window of time between my grandfather's death, when I was eight, and my grandmother's, when I was twelve, I was performing my usual school reluctance on a miserable morning. My grandmother said, "Grandpa would want you to go to school." I was stunned, and I was furious. I remember blurting out, through tears, "That's not fair." To betray the living, or belittle or confront them, that was one thing. But how could one deny or disobey the dead? My mother did not step in and respond to my fury at this manipulation, and I almost hated her for it. My two most potent memories of my grandfather were standing in his kitchen, which, in a prism of spatial irony, was to become my bedroom after my grandparents' deaths, and standing near the cupboards in the morning, eating creamed herring out of the jar on broken-off pieces of matzo; and being taught to wipe the head of my penis with a piece of toilet paper so it didn't drip. But Max was, and this has been further embellished since, a generally elegant and mysterious memory for me. My grandfather Max the tailor, whose clothes, especially in photographs of him in his twenties and thirties, showed a kind of suited elegance that I crafted into my most enduring sartorial inheritance.

Perhaps I *needed* to betray my mother, to turn away from her unassuming, overwhelming, gently suffocating attention. I needed to lose her to find myself, at least this is what I think was playing out; the family romance had to curdle, and I was just the fellow for the job. I stopped accepting her food, making my own low-fat plates of fruit and cottage cheese, yogurt, raw vegetables, broth. She was stunned, not just by my rejection of food, but, in fact, by my gradual rejection of her. I couldn't bear to be physically touched by her, this in a family that kissed hellos and good-byes when we went to check the mail. I grew testy — every other word was "What?!" as though I couldn't understand the most basic logic of what she might be saying to me. With each pound lost, and thirty came off in the first month, my sullen withdrawal and intolerance increased until each new lost pound greeted her like a slap across the face. I came to be so disgusted with her, with what I perceived as a kind of sickening softness, a grotesque solicitude, that I ended up exchanging physical self-loathing for emotional self-detestment. The look on her face whenever I turned down food was a kind of understanding devastation.

My body lies . . .

The rest of the weight came off in a month or two, and my weight fluctuated in a ten-pound range or so for most of the next twenty years. There are photographs of me in my midtwenties, in unsparingly bright Texas light, in which I look rather bloated. From thirty-five to forty I seemed to have mastered thinness somewhat definitively, rarely surpassing one hundred and thirty-five pounds. I never allowed my mother to get very close again, although I tried and came close in the last year of her life.

I flew to New York from California just before going on to the next stages of a job I had recently begun, of all things a study on how children experience pain. My surprise visit was due to Rhoda's month-long diagnosis of "walking pneumonia." I caught the red-eye and stayed that way for a year. We had a day of playing gin rummy and drinking coffee and smoking cigarettes around the kitchen table, a sweet consoling scene for both of us, before I accompanied her to the doctor, whose new diagnosis was more ominous. Cancer or tuberculosis. He did some tests, would know in two days. The family rallied around tuberculosis like a favorite hometown sports team. I delayed my return to California; the news came back—we lost. At the end of *The Magnificent Seven*, Yul Brynner says, "We lose. We always lose." That's the way diagnoses and prognoses go. It's always bad. If I had a garden full of dark prognoses blooming every spring, I'd cut them all back and take my chances on what would grow by itself. Within a few months, having moved back to New York to help tend my mother, who was sprouting tumors like a malignant greenhouse, I spent my days chauffeuring my mother and father from Brooklyn to Manhattan and back, a series of doctors and hospitals; I was running, smoking like a fiend, and fasting; we were doing all we could to fatten my mother up, which never seemed to work. Just when you can have everything you ever wanted to eat, but were afraid would make you zaftig, everything loses its flavor.

She died. Brooklyn's body sagged, jaundiced and exhausted.

When I was twenty-three, Cathy came to live with me in New York. We had been friends and lovers when I was in graduate school and then while working in Northern California. After I had moved back east, she came to visit, and over a six- or seven-day period in Manhattan, we were goners. I flew west to fly east with her, the first day of winter, 1980. My mother died two weeks later; photos of me that spring all capture the same strange, wan look: lovesick and sick with the loss of love. But the strangest thing for me about living in Manhattan with Cathy was how odd, how novel it was to be loved by, loving, and seen with a beautiful woman. I was sure people, especially men, were looking at us in restaurants and thinking *What is she doing with him*. I gradually became used to this, would occasionally feel almost attractive. But mostly I would think *I am a very ordinary looking man who is capable of entrapping the love of beautiful women. What an entirely strange idea.*

My compulsions would never again be as compulsive, as secretly satisfying. The body I bore spent years in repetitive behaviors, pushing and pulling, Montaigne and Descartes arm-wrestling over whether the body should be indulged or dismissed. All it led to was a kind of Swiftian disgust with the entire question. Neither the body nor the mind, which were beginning to consider each other in complexly interesting ways, did so with much gusto. Perhaps because Brooklyn was full of so much bittersweet food, I was indigestible for many years, couldn't even self-cannibalize in any way that felt remotely near grace and gracefulness. Not that I had ever experienced either, nor am I sure I have yet, but one would think that when a body dies, when something is lost, there is the chance for redemption, that shocks to the system can at least provoke change. My tone is darkening, I see, because I'm not sure where I am, in this essay, or in this body. My diction is yearning for a body of language that can tell me not only what has happened, but why I still feel so hungry for the past, as though if I ate it whole, swallowed the outline of a rejected body, a missed mother, a place whose name is my favorite word to say, as though Brooklyn's body were a host placed on my tongue, tart and hard, full of inexplicable pleasures, some dark, like bitter chocolate, others like the first bite of ripe summer melons.

I haven't wanted to leave these subjects, so mixed with pain and pleasure, so central to forty years of living in the flesh. And it's soothing, in a sense, to have them become words, whose bodies seem more reasonable, more manageable, whose corruption I have handled with more dignity. I have never asked words to tell me that I'm good, or have a pretty face, or that I can give a surfeiting pleasure. With language I've had a fairly stable relationship — I've tried to not promise I could give it more, nor have I ever wanted to give it less than was in my power. If I have, on occasion, seduced words for the sake of trying to fill an old wound, in the end I have always found language too resilient and indifferent to being so used, and ended up a reformed verbal lothario. If my subject here is an early body that refuses to leave — the body that came to dinner — which has been protean and parasitic and very much maligned, perhaps it will be contained in the body of this essay, having been given a kind of testimony, having been fed. But I doubt it. The hunger of memory, as Richard Rodriguez suggests, is insatiable.

I love to eat, and it is still something of a torment. I savor and suffer each treat I indulge. I like the cigarette I light after a meal just slightly more than all the others I smoke. Last week I bought a corded silk Gucci shirt the color of wine, on sale at Saks Fifth Avenue. It makes me look so slim, elegant when combined with worsted-wool black pants with a slight shine, a pair of ankle-high boots. On Saturday, before going out to dinner at a local Italian restaurant, famous for nothing but excessive olive oil, I put on my finery and stood swinging myself slowly in the decked-out circle. I checked the mirror and was almost half-pleased — fully hungry, but alert to the damage that a single meal might do, the wrong food brought to the lips.

Distant Voice

remember waking with a start, noticing the time on my digital clock — 7:14 — and standing up on my platform bed. I stepped lively over my sleeping lover and bounded to the table where the ringing phone lay. I expected to be told that my mother was dead; she had been degenerating for months from her cancer's ubiquity, the days lately full of lugubrious increments, small steps toward the inevitable. My father's voice said, "David, Mother is dead." I said, "What?" in soft astonishment, though I had heard. I had heard him clearly. My father said, "You heard me, Mother is dead." He said this rather testily. I was struck by his use of "Mother," a term of generic authority that my brother and I never used. "Mother" and "Father" were something Katharine Hepburn would say in *The Philadelphia Story* or *Holiday*. One addresses one's mother as "Mother" in Cape Cod or Martha's Vineyard. Somewhere like that. Not in Brooklyn. It was as though my father had, so aptly, conceptualized the event for me: she died and took the archetype, the icon, with her. But I felt an immense distance from him, from the fact.

I was calm when I woke my lover and told her the news. It was strange hearing of the death of one woman I loved, then seeming to bring another to life, a fairy-tale inversion. I was calm on the ride from Manhattan to Brooklyn; I had the presence of mind to fix on the irony of riding the D train to the scene of death. I was calm when I met my brother and father at the door of the house. We embraced; we did not cry. Nor did I cry, though rendered breathless, nightmare-breathless and dizzy, when I spied my mother in her house-dress, head swaddled in a kerchief, one eye half open, lying on the bathroom floor.

My grief blossomed on the telephone. The male triumvirate had assigned themselves phone tasks: bearers of bad news. I called Louise, the mother of an old friend. She had known me since I was eight, but the years had thrown their weight behind long lapses in our acquaintance. She picked up the phone; I told her the news, a model of succinct delivery. She said, "Oh, David . . . ," in a paroxysm, releasing my own, creating a kind of chorus. The sound of our names never loses its aura of possibilities.

In addition to the force of her effusion, my "unlocking" was the voice of this mother on the phone, reminding me of the voice that was gone, whose quality had already begun leaking into diffusion. Before I moved back to New York from California, my relationship with my mother was focused, dependent on the phone, and had been for years. The disembodied voice of comfort did comfort, though right up until the time of her death I had kept her at arm's length. Her voice — gentle, emotive, a classic New York accent softened by her early years in rural New Jersey — usually elicited a cold, somewhat formal response in an accent of cultivated academic flatness.

The tension between distance and proximity has always seemed to me a crucial characteristic of phone talk. Proximity is the familiar voice, synecdoche of the person we are talking to. We take our own voices for granted on the phone, call on others to recognize us by them without identification. When we catch a hesitation in the answering voice, we ask in a kind of jesting apprehension, "Do you know who this is?" and feel slightly rebuffed, as though our voices aren't distinctive enough, or we are excluded from the circle of voices who speak for themselves, the inner circle of the most important. Proximity also involves possibility. I have good friends in distant places whom I speak to a few times a year, but I could talk to them anytime, any time I need or want to. In such cases the telephone acts as a kind of preserving solution; it obviates the need for consistent contact. In this, of course, there is a price. The price of potential is the constant future tense, permanent procrastination. I was painfully aware of possibility when I received the early morning call from my father. I could have talked to my mother ten minutes earlier, interrupting her ablutions for death, her death. I could have reached her disembodied voice; all I was left with was her disembodied life.

Part of the distance of voice on the telephone has to do with the absence of the visual cues that normally accompany vocal gesture. Even between people of the greatest familiarity, the chance of missed sarcasms, missed nuances, misinterpretation, is constant. Yet the way our bodies disappear on the phone can be a relief, a boon. I remember asking out a girl named Frieda in my junior year of high school. She was shapely, wore glasses, and voiced an appreciation of George Mc-Govern, all qualities I had much admiration of. I wanted to take her to a concert for McGovern at Madison Square Garden. To ease my "phonervousness," I shut off all of the lights on the first floor of our house, where my brother and I had our rooms. I dialed the number with a pen-sized flashlight and crouched against the wall to await the moment of my well-rehearsed request. Frieda did not go with me, then or ever ("My boyfriend wouldn't approve," she said), but the darkness was a way of turning myself into pure voice. The idea of body and voice calling voice seemed a disadvantage. By effecting the obliteration of my body, I was establishing metaphysical equanimity. I wanted to be less real, less there. Need I add I was a painfully self-conscious teenager? I was a brief year or two past technical obesity. Turning the lights off for Frieda completed the half-darkness of phone talk. And it might have been those few moments that convinced me of the difference between what happens in the dark and what happens in the light, any light.

In 1965 my mother took me to the New York World's Fair. There was a room full of "products of the future," among them the "T.V.-phone." My mother and I went into separate rooms and talked, and looked at each other. Many of the items in that room, the once-futuristic, have since become commonplace, but no one ever talks about the "T.V.-phone." One reason, I suggest, is that adding picture to voice would vitiate the essence of the telephone, destroy the necessary physical anonymity we rely upon, and make talking on the phone a much less intimate experience. Pictures tend to dominate words. I recall my mother's face, the absence of self-conscious discomfort. I remember her bouffant hairdo, but nothing of what she said.

We rely upon physical anonymity on the phone, even if we usually do not deny the body completely. Think of the things you do on the phone that you would never do in front of anyone under any circumstances. It makes the act of phoning a wonderfully disjunctive experience: "You did? I'm so happy for you!" (finger deeply probing the ear). In addition, we can do things like run over and grab a cigarette (run out and grab a cigarette if confronted with a monologue) while the person we are talking to, casual acquaintance or closest friend, drones on, a model of the soporific. We run back in time to say, "Huh?" or "Uh-huh" or "Really?"

I would receive weekly calls from my mother when I lived in California, spending most of my time in a dark studio apartment in Palo Alto. I was grateful any time the phone would ring. My connection to the outside world, which I rarely saw, was tenuous. But I would affect boredom when she called, as though I were in the middle of something fascinating I yearned to return to.

Now when I think of our voices mystically channeled into some sort of impulse, propelled thousands of miles, only to be reassembled in their original structures of pain, I experience a different yearning, not at all distant.

Who knows what lay behind Bell's first phone words: "Watson, come here, I need you." Maybe the small distance, room to room, allowed Bell to tell Watson what he had been longing to admit. Maybe that need was the inspiration for the invention of the telephone. Perhaps the most telling acknowledgment of that need is what we say when we lose it, when it is taken out of our hands, beyond our control. We say the line went dead.

Further Father: Remembering John Waterman

 paradox: when I try to think of the most generic name imaginable, I think past John Smith (a tiny graduate student I served with somewhere in the disarmed forces of academia), Tom Brown (whose schooldays intrude on the common names of my schooldays: Schwartzes and Petrocellis), and John Doe (a name I've always found both silly and elegant, whose etymology I've wondered about with the idle curiosity that does not send one on etymological crusades) to John Waterman, a name I find singularly bland, but which nominally resonated throughout my childhood through my teenage years. John Waterman was my father.

Sort of. John Waterman was my father's pseudonym, pragmatically crafty alter ego, his all-purpose floating other who served us well through his many guises, positions, familiarities, and resources.

Last month, back to New York for a visit, I was making reservations at a midtown restaurant for my father and stepmother, brother and sister-in-law, and myself. My father hovered nearby: "Make it in the name of John Waterman," he said, with a genial smirk. I did so. Old scams die hard.

My father's name is Leo Lazar, a name I've never grown tired of, as though the swift syllabic balance, the semantic suggestion of lion and leper, embodied the Runyonesque vitality, operatic temper, bad joke–spilling, egocentric generosity of this man I've known for forty years. My brother and I had a joke, in adolescence, that still tells. In the midst of our greatest dread at our father's anger (which we had seen reduce grown women to sobs, grown men to inward-pulling, dark unresponsiveness bordering on despair), we would refer to him secretly as Leola Czar. Leo La Czar might have done the trick — we were, after all, descended from turn-of-the-century refugees from Nicholas II,

Waterman at work.

on my mother's side — except for the fact that the preservation of my father's first name failed to convey the metamorphic quality he achieved in rage. Leola, though feminine sounding, captured the *Arabian Nights* strangeness of the dervish who would spew out invective when provoked. And it didn't take much. But, fantasies aside, my father has always been Leo Lazar, that quick alliterative combination with the pleasurable effect of a left hook; it rises and falls on its vowels, and then it's over. My friends take pleasure in saying the name, and if I alternate between references to my father and to Leo in this essay, it is because I think of him both as my kindred source of all sources, and as a slightly avuncular character who is sometimes quite escapable, quick with a riposte, loudspoken, eager to retell a joke (I prefer the strangeness of the ones with a Yiddish punch line, since it puts the joke a bit out of reach and into a cultural realm I feal affection for, albeit distance from).

It's perhaps difficult for some to imagine the cultural difference between first-generation parents raised in the Depression, and second-generation teenagers raised in the sixties. My father's parents had escaped pogroms in Austria and Romania to come to New York at the turn of the century. My grandfather was a small, silent man who spent fifty years working his way from waiter to busboy, mostly at New York's then-host of "dairy" restaurants, beat kosher family places that have all but vanished. Ratner's, on Delancey Street, hangs on still, but every visit there, performed at four- or five-year intervals, frequently as a cultural service to my usually non-Jewish girlfriend of the time, confirms that any given trip back may be the last. It languishes in a half-hearty way. My father was a smart kid, by all accounts. Quick-witted, astute, academically inclined simply by quickness of mind rather than extreme diligence. He whizzed through school. Can any word, I wonder, be further from the Yiddish my father grew up with than "whizzed"? "Is there anything further, Father?" Zeppo Marx asks Groucho in *Horsefeathers*, in which Groucho plays the college president, Zeppo his collegiate athlete son. Groucho's retort: "That can't be right. Isn't it anything fa(r)ther further?"

My father graduated high school at fifteen — in the graduation photos he looks like a twelve-year-old greenhorn. Right off the boat and into the cap and gown. Strange, for a Jewish immigrant family, what happened next. My father was awarded a scholarship to Cornell University. He intended, he tells me, to study animal husbandry, which boggles my mind, considering that my only experience of my father and animals consists of his railing for fifteen years at the cow-shaped fox terrier that soiled and befouled our shag carpets with impunity, and the memory of a family busting out laughing at the Miami Monkey Jungle, circa 1962, when a large ape ceremoniously looked my father in the eye and slowly turned, spread her cheeks, and offered a rosy view of its world.

My father offered to get a job in the wake of his own father's depressing (I believe it would last forty or fifty years) depression, and the family, meaning his mother, unexpectedly accepted. A note here (Mr. Waterman, hold the phone, I haven't forgotten you): my father's family was an uncertain matriarchy. My grandmother, Minnie, whom I remember unfondly as shrill, obese, given to operatic sighs preceding opera-length monologues on her proximity to departed relatives (she would join them thirty years later), seemed to have the last word in the family. My father speaks of her younger generosity, holding a large ex-tended family together, providing for them with difficulty while my grandfather, Benny, brought home the pitiful tips left by other pitifully marginal men. Perhaps. He also apparently had a bit of a gambling problem, hard as it is for me to imagine that man with the visage of Elmer Fudd and the personality of Roadrunner — beep beep, sit in the chair and light another stogie — doing anything that smacks of obsession. Considering this information, though, I have been treated on several occasions to one of the strangest lines I've ever heard in the context of family historiographies; when I've asked my father about his family's financial situation, he has frequently told me that his mother felt that his father "pissed all his money away on cigars." Am I missing something? A pittance on poker and a fortune on cheap sweets? How much can one man smoke? The line that got Groucho taken off the air, said to a female guest who said that she had seven children and that her husband operated a screwing machine: "Look, lady, I like my cigar, but even I take it out sometimes." I have images of a Jewish Elmer Fudd in dreamland, tattered pajamas, a beaten-up mattress, sounds of the street picking up the metal taste of a tenement iron fire-escape on a hot Orchard-Street night, a thin plume of smoke escaping from the lit cigar, puffing alternating with snoring. It's possible that in my father's mind, what his mother told him as avoidance or euphemism for gambling, cigars, took on a parallel explanatory function, cigars and gambling. I mean, after all, he probably smoked while he dealt or tossed. Or perhaps I just hold onto the phrase for the unlikely combination of "pissed" and "cigars," which would seem to cancel one another out. In any case, my father skipped college, went to work at a travel agency, and then a ribbon company for the next eight years until Pearl Harbor. They treated him well in the ribbon business. He cut the mustard. Will there be anything further, Father? You bet your life.

The affinity of this question to where am I. I was making dinner reservations in the name of John Waterman. My father had a John Waterman phone in his office, and when my brother and I worked for my father's travel agency, mostly answering phones or running errands, we were under strict orders to answer this phone, "John Waterman's office. Can I help you?" John Waterman was protean. Sometimes he was Mayor Lindsay's commissioner for cultural affairs, sometimes a representative of the State Department. Occasionally, he was vice president of Pan Am or TWA. Once in a while he was even more exotic, Monaco's ambassador to the United Nations, or enigmatic: chairman of Waterman Enterprises or Sebring Limited. He was whatever was perceived as necessary to achieve whatever was perceived as needed, with my father as the Alec Guinness of the travel industry, playing all parts.

The Waterman phone was in two small offices, successively, both belonging to Comet Travel Service, the travel agency my father opened in 1962 with the proceeds of his settlement with Seagate Travel, of which he had been a partner. What I remember about Seagate is lust for a ferris wheel. In the foyer of this office was a mechanical ferris wheel, sturdily constructed of metal and painted wood, whose tiny seats, passengerless, were always in motion. I never failed to ooh and ahh over it when I visited my father at the office. And he never failed to not let me have it. This, I believe, since I remember it as a rather elaborate and expensive machine, was no doubt a good lesson in patience and denial that I feel rather unambiguously set against in the pantheon of lessonship. What's the good of denial, after all, if there's no payoff? I blame a certain tendency to immediately gratify on this elusive early wheel. When the partnership ended litigiously — my father's partners tried to cut him out, and my father thought he was ruined until a careful reading of the ownership contract revealed that Leo's signature had to be on checks forced a favorable settlement — I felt that a bad deal had been struck since my father did not take the wheel with him.

In the search for a name for the new agency, my legacy of cleverness in the family was dubiously enshrined by gazing at a can of Comet soap powder and suggesting that as a name for the agency since, and there is genius in this, comets are fast. A clever lad. A remarkable lad. I could have fetched a Christmas-morning goose for Scrooge.

So the new agency took shape with John Waterman as my father's general partner. The travel business was a different animal in those days before deregulation. There was, shall we say, a more subdued level of scrutiny. The airline food chain was complicated by upstarts, but dominated instead by the well-fed likes of Pan Am, TWA, United. Pan Am and TWA had a special aura as international carriers. The supervisors at Kennedy International Airport, which was in transition from the slightly sprawling Idlewild to the disorganized behemoth it has become, had enormous power to decide who got on what flight and at what class, who got bumped, who was ushered into the first-class lounge. I remember, especially, Joe Girardi at TWA. Joe was thirty-fiveish, handsome, smooth, vaguely associated with the mob, although this was never pressed. When my brother or I would ask my father about this (why we asked about this, other than the fact that we lived blocks from Gambino, and Joe was Italian, I'm not sure), my father would answer vaguely: Joe knows a lot of people. Joe waltzed through TWA's terminal, that sleek and slanted fifties bit of modernism, which never failed to impress me as a child as being entirely "space age," as though he owned the joint. I remember one of my father's repeated questions: I've got Sid Liebman from Novelty Imports on the 248 to Rome. He's a big guy. What can you do? What could be done was to upgrade him, and the games would begin. Joe would get tough seats on a different airline for a friend or associate, or an all-but-impossible Christmas room at the San Juan Hotel in Puerto Rico. Liebman would reward my father: five boxes of dresses for my mother, undoubtedly a bit of cash — less than the first-class ticket would cost, but not small change. There were tons of these transactions; one hand was washing the other so much that a general state of manual hygiene might have been declared.

Joe was unusual for my father's airline contacts in that he crossed the border into family friend. He seemed to have unlimited sports contacts, and I couldn't begin to count the times when we sat with him at New York Jets and Giants games. He moved in a kind of subcelebrity world, hanging out with second-string linebackers, third-rate entertainers, City Hall managers, businessmen, stewardesses, wise guys. And he was a swell guy, solicitous always to my brother and me. It was occasionally confusing as a kid to realize that my favorite of my father's associates, the ones who were genuinely nicest, were frequently the shadiest. There was a crooked courtliness to these men that seemed to be engaged by smart kids, as though we, scholastically inclined but not eggheads, had a chance to go the up-and-up route, college and such, that they mostly had not followed.

My father's business was focused almost entirely on the garment district, just up Seventh Avenue from his office on Thirty-third Street, across from Madison Square Garden. But his contacts, and I suspect his reputation as being the guy to call when there was a "tough ticket," brought some celebrities his way, too, whose names he would then use, cautiously and strategically: calling ahead to the airline lounge (if he didn't have a contact there) as John Waterman, Tony Bennett's advance man, or telling the Garden that Bill Dana — remember Jose Jimenez? — was in town and wanted to see *Mame*, or more unlikely, Janis Joplin. I recall strolling with my father down Fifth Avenue — unlikely; I should amend that to walking less than light speed, since the stroll was a pedestrian dance as foreign to my family's movement as Mexican food or mayo with roast beef was to our cuisine. My father and I cantered down Fifth Avenue, a rather more relaxed venue on a summer weekend in 1962 than it seems today, and were in front of Saks when my father and a casually dressed gentleman greeted each other warmly. I looked up and said hello. I mostly remember we were standing next to a spittoon. As we moved on, my father said, "That was Perry Como." He might as well have said Major Duomo, but I know that I was supposed to be impressed.

One time when I anticipated the thrall of stardom with unprecedented glee, it turned instead to a rather heady gall. My father was taking me to the airport to meet Danny Kaye. I must have been ten or eleven. And he was taking just me — no distracting brother to bother with. Danny Kaye was the sine qua non of stars to me then. His pitch in movies like *The Secret Life of Walter Mitty* or *A Connecticut Yankee in King Arthur's Court* was perfect to the tune of smart ten- to twelve-year-olds; he combined, after all, the flustered impotence of someone who can't seem to get the world right, with the escaping luck of the modestly wisecracking schlemiel hero. Perfect; certainly perfect for me. I was clever, inward-growing, and my middle names were Run Away. My father had booked him on an elaborate trip, no doubt a tough nut. By this time my father's connections were not only ubiquitous, but he was doing so much business with the airlines that he could invoke more direct front-scene clout.

We pulled into the parking space of one of the vice presidents of TWA, behind the building, where the spilling garbage always seemed to give the lie to, at the very least diminish the luster of, sweeping futuristic arches. If a security cop asked, John Waterman was parking in Mr. Wright's spot by permission. Just ask him.

In the center of the terminal, near the giant black international departures screen, was a tight little crowd. A bulb or two popped. The tight circle of celebrity was unmistakable. And it was rather appropriate for the star to settle under the departures screen. After all, I loved it, too. When we would go to Kennedy, sometimes two or three times a week, I could be entertained no better than to be deposited in front of that screen, its clackety-clack changes announcing a change or departure to Lisbon or Dresden, Rome or Rio. It seemed so exotic even the times became charged — not just Rome, but flight 764, at 4:52, every number a talisman, a numerological clue to places far from Brooklyn, places where people moved languorously, spoke in vesperal whispers, and drank iced tea all the livelong day. No doubt that's where Danny Kaye was going, and this being the midsixties, I had no visions of sultry lasses awaiting his star-bored lassitude — no Larry Olivier in drag for this baby.

We penetrated the circle of admirers like a knife through butter, and walked up to Danny Kaye. Leo said, "Danny, hi, this is my son David." I said, "How do you do, Mr. Kaye," and he smiled and bent down to one knee. His smile held and he gazed into my eyes. Was I to be drawn into the mysterious aura of fame? I think instead I had the thrill of a potential recognition moment. I just knew at that instant that Danny Kaye was seeing something in me that I had always known was there, but that no one else could perceive. It was a Special Quality.

This is what Danny Kaye whispered to me: "Now, you know you shouldn't be so chubby. Next time I see you I want you to have taken off some of that weight." Perhaps the self-improvement movement begins with this moment, almost thirty years ago. But I doubt it. I said okay, and was thinking, and this is where Brooklyn always came in handy: what a complete shmuck. Walter Mitty stood up without any idea of the secret life of epithets he had inspired. What did he say, my father asked me, touched that I had been given such gentle attention. He told me to lose weight. My father was a bit surprised and a bit amused. My brother was very amused, and used Danny Kaye against me until I shed my pounds of Danny-flesh. My mother thought it cruel and tactless. Points for Mom. So much for the Kid from Brooklyn.

I had a similar experience with George Maharis, also at TWA. He had starred in *Route 66*, and a film I remember thinking was interesting called *The Spider's Stratagem*. *Route 66* was way cool, so I was looking forward to this meeting in the first-class lounge, hope springing eternal. Maharis was eating and apologized for it. He was terribly friendly and gregarious. Asked the right questions: Yankees or Mets, what about those Celtics. He pulled out an equally gregarious photograph — I remember him smiling and waving in it. This is what he wrote: "For David — I bet I can eat more than you can. Next time I see you we'll have an eating contest. Think you can beat me?" He may not have meant this as an insult, but I found a second reference to rotundity unprofound and depressing, even if it was well intentioned. Brushes with greatness — Danny Kaye, Perry Como, George Maharis, and others. Already I was plotting a life of anonymity, sensitivity, and thinness.

John Waterman was not a real star, but he always came up with the cache. I decided early on, despite a twinge or two when first exposed to the concept of paternal . . . shall we say moral complexity? But I learned early to accept the reigning pragmatism of this and other arrangements since I was so clearly their beneficiary, even though they struck me once in a while as ignoble, and sometimes as humiliating. When I was eight and we flew, I was booked as age two. At twelve I was five, and at fifteen I was eight. I was the largest but slowest chronologically advancing human being in Brooklyn. My brother and I were sometimes told to "make yourselves scarce" at the airport, lest the ticket agent in Miami or Nassau think we were not on the up-and-up. But I got to go a lot of places. And I learned, even if I never quite mastered the trick of it, to sound sure of the scam you're pulling. It really does work wonders. Perhaps this made me a proficient liar, in a casual sense. Perhaps it helped make me a writer.

I witnessed many of my father's telephone transactions as Waterman. For some reason, each persona was accompanied by an accent. My father particularly liked invoking some variant of the flat Midwestern or generically Southern accent for Waterman. That this worked sometimes puzzled me. Why would Mayor Wagner's special assistant be from Des Moines or Tuscaloosa? As I grew older, I would sometimes wince at what seemed so accentually stereotypical as to be unbelievable. And I wondered at my father's inner workings, what the accent was internally, when he invoked this floating persona and the voices that accompanied it.

Accent seems to have figured largely in my life, my own and others. I like the word, which in its verb and adverbial forms connotes an interesting take on emphasis, slightly less dominant, but figuring prominently, as when one accents a stew with spices, or ac-cent-uates the positive. My adult accent emerged from an attempt to eliminate the negative, as I perceived it. I had a rather heavy Brooklyn accent as a kid, mostly picked up from my mother, who had a classic B-movie doozy of a Brooklyn accent, almost worthy of Jean Hagen in *Singing in the Rain* ("I can't *stand* him"), despite growing up in rural New Jersey until she was fourteen or so.

I first became aware of my accent in a speech class in eighth grade. My teacher was Mrs. Padow, one of those large-bosomed normal-school types who, at the age of fifty-five or so, had managed to cultivate an air of boredom that would do justice to the shallow existentialist of your choice. Once, in an attempt to impress her, I told her that I had been reading Bernard Malamud's novels. "Yes, yes," she replied abstractly, "he writes very nice children's books." I resisted correcting her for two reasons: 1) I was not the correcting type; I was the make-a-note-of-that type, equal parts polite and introverted; and 2) what would it have mattered? She obviously didn't care, so I couldn't very well tell her what she already both knew and didn't know. She knew she was wasting our time and hers, so why should she have cared about Bernard Malamud?

We all had to memorize and recite several speeches for this class. There was no clear pedagogical explanation for this; it was simply what we did. And, indeed, I'm grateful, since I remember everything I recited. My first toeing of the recitation line was near-traumatic; worse, it was baffling. I had chosen the classic soliloquy from Macbeth: "Tomorrow and tomorrow and tomorrow. . . ." I spoke the first line, and at every *and* the entire class spontaneously burst out into a mocking exaggeration of my pronunciation. *Eeeund*, they kept repeating. I had no idea what was going on for a moment or two, until I realized that they were mocking my accent. This is a very strange memory for me to consider, since no matter how strong my accent may have been, it's difficult to believe that theirs was not equally strong, or even more, shall we say, pronounced. Was it, I wonder, a moment of recognition, even self-consciously, that managed to escape their understanding? They kidded me about it for days, and I could see the look of anticipation when my next turn came — I had chosen Puck's last speech this time. But by this time the *a*'s had softened with my own self-consciousness, beginning a process that would accelerate when I went to college.

I went to an expensive, somewhat experimental college in New England. All right, I went to Bennington. I've always had an excuse to be a bit queasy about that. First it was the years of responses beginning "I thought that was a girls' school," one of those idiotic responses akin to "I thought you were dead." What was I supposed to say, "Yes, it is, but I look great in drag"? After that, thanks to a *Time* article, my inquisitors would angle their heads and smirk out, "Isn't that the most expensive school in the country?" It was for a time, and I went there thanks to my father's generosity and John Waterman's many successful enterprises. My father flatly told me that I could go to any school I chose, a gesture completely endearing and more than understandable from one who didn't get to go at all. These days, my embarrassment about Bennington is more direct: I hate the manipulative faculty-bashing moves of its current administration. If a school exists on a kind of fraternity with its alumni, I disown it.

But I was never completely owned by it. I was one of the outsiders there: ethnic, uncool, studious, and still with a wash of Brooklyn in the accent. But I made it my business to get rid of it. I took voice lessons from a man who had an almost cultlike following; he was a longtime faculty member who had had a stroke and communicated in whispers. Singing lessons were like vespers. One had to concentrate, and there was, for many, a kind of sacred aura about studying singing and voice from a man who could not perform the former and could barely produce the latter. He kept missing my diaphragm in individual lessons, straying so low that the odds of a mere mistaken brush of the hand seemed impossible. Twice I bellowed "No" at him, the way one would upbraid an unruly dog or a straying child. This ended my singing career, which was marked with a fine vibrato only when I was nervous enough to produce it unnaturally.

But, privately, I kept refining my accent, moderating my vowels, softening my consonants. A friend at the time said I sounded like an English don. That must have been my progression from Brooklyn don. Corleone to Cambridge, made easily.

But this wasn't a dark obsession, the need to rid myself of background and blend it. It was more specific than that, clearly, since my greatest joy at Bennington was dinner with Roy Weinberg. We had about the same demographic profile, other than the fact that he had moved to Manhattan from the Bronx as an adolescent. We would meet in what I called the Pariah dining room, one of the smaller halls, off to the side.

The blue bloods didn't venture there. But even the ragtag lot who did were sometimes quieted and disquieted by the conversations Roy and I had: boisterous, improvisatory, and full of the Lower East Side. We would talk like two old clothing merchants, invoke the doggerel of Mott Street, praising our far background by mockingly invoking it. We would have felt, on a rather profound level, that "Tell me what street/Compares with Mott Street/In July" had an irony that was entirely gentle.

"So, how's business?"

"Metza, metza. It comes, it goes."

"You got new suits?"

"I got new suits. What else I'm gonna get if not new suits?"

"It's a question, all right? Not necessary to put on a shigun."

That kind of thing. We howled. We liked seeming unsophisticatedly devoted to our backgrounds. But we both also developed rather flat elocutionary styles, slower, dappled with irony, as opposed to bursting with the sarcasm we had grown up with. Both of our ways paid by fathers who had made good: made good money. We could be of our background, or, in the larger world, unplaceable rather than implacable. If Leo had ruses that brought in the bucks and got us the tough tickets, then I had my own ruse: I could assimilate perfectly, when I wanted to. My culture was something I invoked when comfortable. Otherwise, I became other wise. I was so savvy that the only possible way to exist seemed to me to be enigmatic, persona-empowered. I enjoyed the guessing games about where I was from when I met someone. I suppose I thought I was winning something.

At times, there clearly seemed to be some pleasure on Leo's part at the success of his ruses; a small smile would creep across his face-as-Waterman, a smile that seemed to indicate the satisfaction of the scam — the practical joke with a material payoff. I could and can understand this. As a matter of fact, I have, ironically, never trusted anyone who was incapable of "putting one over," as though the inability to be obviously untrustworthy at least some of the time bespeaks a moral weakness, or thinness of character. But how much deeper and in what other directions did my father's satisfaction go? This is speculation on my part, but I wonder about the mantle of "the other" he was donning, what that felt like. Living Jewish in New York can be very

comfortable and hermetic, true, but my father had certainly had his experiences "out there." He had been in the service in Oklahoma and
India when, despite the host of war movies with the bespectacled,
eggheaded, and more or less accepted Jewish serviceman as a standard
type, he must have encountered veritable worlds of otherness unpro-
tected by the surrounding cushion of familiarity he had had, and would
have, in New York. Was there a frisson of transgression in being a temporary goy?

My father told me a story recently that I had never heard. He was in
the service waiting for assignment overseas. I believe it was for a
couple of months in Tennessee, circa 1942. He started dating a young
local woman named Virginia, the name itself a far cry from Lower
Broadway, and an incriptive redoubling of his journey south of Mason
and Dixon. His description of the affair is rather generic — she was "a
very nice girl and we were in love." And he considered marriage. To
my astonishment, Leo told me that he asked *his* parents for permission. And they declined. "I didn't really want to, but I broke it off. She
was a shiksa and my parents couldn't accept it, and I just couldn't go
against their wishes."

I was stunned by this story. My father is a formidable man: head-
strong, wily, and before the mellowing of his later years, following my
mother's untimely death, full of rage. Rage is a word that should not be
used for merely excessive anger; it denotes a state far enough beyond
anger as to constitute a separate state, a qualitative rather than merely
quantitative difference. And my father held full citizenship. In the
offices of Comet Travel, several times a week, a preternatural quiet
would settle on the dusty desks when my father's telephone explosions
would suck all of the oxygen out of the room. Screaming epithets into
the phone ear of some airline functionary — frequently prefaced by
"Never in my life . . ." — Leo as Leo would reduce the target of his
rage to single-cellular status. Sometimes these would be followed with
mild apologies to the supervisors who had performed whatever service it was my father was, shall we say, requesting, usually, however, accompanied by a disclaimer that indicated that the outburst would not
have been necessary if he or she had known what to do: serve. I would
get very queasy during these episodes, having been the target myself
any number of times. My father, these days, likes to tell the story of
when I was implored by my mother, that sweet Jewish intercessor, to

go in and apologize to my father before bed for whatever infraction had been performed or perceived. I did so, reluctantly, hangdog. My father launched into a rather vituperative lecture on my worthlessness. My endgame response, sullen but somewhat brave, considering what I was up against, was: "I just wanted to say I'm sorry." My father tells this story with a very mild and implicit self-mockery. I am far from unsympathetic; having achieved a free and funny, a speak-your-mind and kibitzing kinship with my near-dotage dad, I grow weary and bored at the idea of stashing and rehashing wounds as a lugubrious form of postponed adolescent entertainment. I keep them, for literary purposes, to my essays. I don't need to work much out with a smart survivor of an old man who has, all things considered, been rather good to me. Nevertheless, or is it be that as it may, I did experience a withering, what sometimes felt apocalyptic, dressing down with disturbing frequency in my childhood and adolescence.

Remember, I got over it. But it took a while to understand, forget, transcend, whatever it was I did. There was the time, for example, when Leo, in a rage upstairs, screamed to my mother's witness ears that he didn't love my brother and me, and probably never had. My brother, Scott, and I were hunched silently on the stairs, eavesdropping, if such a thing is possible at dangerous decibel levels. We never discussed this moment. Once, I believe in my early twenties, in the throes of primary therapizing, I mentioned this moment to my father and received a resounding lack of confirmation. To say such things was clearly an impossibility. I have come to accept not only that the debated history of paternal excess is a seminal childhood experience, but also that, past a certain age, confirmation can be a cold comfort. My bones are getting old and need to settle on hard-won familial-historical accuracies very little. But yet, I will tell you I felt rather small and orphaned at that moment. True rage is radical: it can diminish or destroy. I'm more concerned at this moment, though, with the need that fed the urge to diminish, rather than the diminishee.

So my father, a grown man, yielded again to the narrow interests of his parents. The equanimity with which he speaks of this is striking. Of course, considering the happiness of his married life with my mother, I suppose this fragment of the past could be consigned to the happy-accident category. (And lest this characterization seem incongruous in the wake of my previous paragraph, let me say this: our family's problems, such as they were, always did an end run around my father and mother's relationship. At the darkest moments of my unhappiness, or my sense of injustice at my father's temporary insanities or my mother's defense of them — "Go apologize" was close to a mantra — I marveled at the equanimity the two of them maintained.) In these versions one can pay homage to old obstacles and injustices that paved the way to moments, scenarios, lives that would not have otherwise been lived. This has always struck me as Panglossian, the blessing of past troubles. For despite the apparent optimism of the outlook is the belief that things couldn't have been better. I mean, the man who falls and breaks his leg and misses the airplane crash today could have changed his flight, saved his leg, and won the lottery, too. I'm leery about giving fate the hail-fellow when I just know he's thinking, *Not so fast — If you only knew*. I'm reminded of the man in Primo Levi's *Survival in Auschwitz*, davening in thanks for having been spared from a selection. Levi's devastating remark, "If I were God I would spit at Kuhn's prayer," strikes me as a terribly sane view of the world. Behind every thank-God-it-wasn't-me is a thank-God-it-was-them, which is, shall we say, uncharitable.

Let me clarify: I really do admire an optimistic view of the past, if that isn't oxymoronic. I just like to see a healthy dose of irony thrown in. But my father is from a less ironic generation. Despite its wonderfully melodramatic dark side, even *The Best Years of Our Lives* ends affirmatively. I mean, we won the war, and most people got houses and sent their kids to college. I really don't mean to be sardonic about this — the older I get, the more I am full of awe and admiration for my parents' generation. I'm not invoking a false fifties consciousness; I'm just tired of my own generation's narcissism when compared to the generation that allowed them to skulk and sulk around with it. And if I have trouble at times understanding my father's own lack of bitterness at his own parents' foibles and follies, perhaps it is because in the slight peering of my own relationship with my father, I feel a bit paternal toward him at times, a bit protective, even about what I consider old wrongs.

John Waterman's protean shadow life, hovering near the telephone, is elusive but not completely escapable. Why *did* Leo choose such a wonderfully generic gentile name in the creation of this "other" Everyman? He says he doesn't remember, picked it out of a hat (Does anyone still wear a hat, as the Sondheim song ruefully asks). But that doesn't hold Waterman for me. For one thing, this nom de telephone had to be a non-Jew, even if these reasons were derived subconsciously. A non-Jewish name would be flexible, useful for both the Jewish and non-Jewish worlds. It would have authority in both. Borough Jews of my father's age were remarkably uninformed about the Christian world, despite the exposure of the war. This was partly willful — a desire to not be contaminated, to not assimilate the culture of Christian America more than was necessary, other than the unavoidable and naturalized but mostly understated presence of it in the media. It was a way of saying *We expect your world to be the world of TV and the movies, more or less, but we're going to try and make believe that Christmas doesn't exist, especially since you simply refuse to acknowledge that Jesus was a nice Jewish boy who went a little soft in the head because of his dubious parentage.* To know more than that, though, I think, was to put oneself in danger of being seduced. There was also some pique involved. After all, *they* know absolutely nothing about us. This sentiment is so strong that it spilled over. Over the years, when I brought a non-Jewish woman home, my father would sometimes act as though she were slightly slow. He would painstakingly instruct her on how to cut a bagel, or ask if she had ever had pastrami, or begin minipaeons to the Jews with something like *The Jews are a very ancient people.* For decorum's sake, I would correct Leo gently, saying something mild and sensitive like, "Jesus Christ, she didn't just step out of the Spaceship Trinity, having come from the planet Shiksa!"

The moxie in the charade was that to be Protestant Mr. Waterman only required certainty, and my father's decades of hard work, a kind of single-minded devotion to what used to be called "building a life," equipped him bountifully with this. Of course, the point is that he was right. In all the years of charades, all the outlandish announcements of position — Waterman as vice president of Nabisco, Waterman as Doris Day's brother, Waterman as England's vice counsel to the United Nations — there was never a slip; the ruse always sailed clear, never foundering on the dubious questions of the rusee. In this my father engaged two bits of fundamental psychology: most workers were too disaffected to care enough to question a status higher than theirs, even if they dared to, which they usually did not; and the knowledge that certainty is convincing. Marlon Brando may have found Lee Strasberg in the early fifties, but he might as well have studied with Leo Lazar. You don't become the character, but it works.

Of course Waterman felt nothing, and I think Leo felt that most people are easily fooled. There must have been some satisfaction in this, some recompense for his own undeveloped education. At eighty-three, my father has lost none of his mental agility, although I sometimes talk to him and sense the wall, the wall of more subtle understandings that an education, or the company of those outside his world, might have led him further toward. He has a healthy and balanced vision of the world, a philosophical streak. It is mixed with fixed ideas and bits of information that are frequently partial, a little too dependent on questionable received information. But Leo knows that I at least will challenge him. He gets a kick out of the way I get riled up when he presents me with what I consider both dubious arguments and statistics in favor of capital punishment. I get a kick out of it too, after I've cooled down. These usually begin on the ride from the airport, somewhere right after how was the flight. Once a few years ago, in the midst of one of these engaging automotive welcomes, I interrupted my father to ask what John Waterman thought of whatever political imbroglio we were entertaining. He said, "Didn't I tell you, Waterman's dead." "Did you go to the funeral?" I inquired. "In a manner of speaking." Touché.

Sometimes I think of John Waterman as the gentile George Kaplan. George Kaplan was a cog in Hitchcock's maguffin, in *North by Northwest*. You may remember it is George Kaplan's name that is being announced when Cary Grant waves to get the attention of the waiter who is calling for Kaplan. The cold-warrior thugs watching from the doorway think Grant is responding to the Kaplan call. Throughout much of the rest of the film, Grant first tries to deny, then plays the role of Kaplan, a very secret agent, so secret in fact that he doesn't even exist. He's a decoy, a name checked into hotels so the good guys (Us, or in Cold War terms, U.S.) can check on the bad guys (Them). But I've always wondered why Ernest Lehmann, the scriptwriter, chose a Jewish name for the decoy. Perhaps he figured that most moviegoers wouldn't recognize it as such, placed it there as a wink to the Jews in the house. But I've sometimes thought of Kaplan as the missing Jew of the fifties, the Jew who didn't die in the camps, or live to tell, who didn't serve and return to Saturday services, but was assimilated away into an empty room, who became the organization man, who became, in one reading, John Waterman, who had been Morris Levine, or Heshy Abramowitz. My father stayed very much a Jew, but needed a chaser of Waterman, an invisible factotum. Perhaps John Waterman helped Leo Lazar stay Leo Lazar, in a sense. John Waterman married the girl down South, and the Orchard Street kids who made it Cornell bought houses in the Hamptons. We lived in Brooklyn and always had the best seats in the house, whether the house was the Eugene O'Neill Theater, Carnegie Hall, or Madison Square Garden.

I had a classmate in elementary school, P.S. 216 in Brooklyn, whose name was James Johnson. He was a Jewish kid, but nonobserving, which was a peculiar phenomenon back then. All the Jewish kids I grew up with went to Hebrew school after regular school for years (not that we learned much of anything there) in gradual preparation for our Bar Mitzvahs. But not James Johnson. And what kind of a name was that? I could piece together the shortened names — Bloom from Bloomberg, Fink from Finkelstein (that was a trade-up?), Lazar from Lazarowitz — but not this one. And James? You might as well smear mayo on your corned beef. My father explained that James Johnson Sr. (another anomaly, since Jews don't name offspring after the living, and therefore the custom of Jrs. and Srs. doesn't exist) worked for a large company that didn't hire many Jews and that this was his way of trying to make it. I was fascinated, and a little disgusted. The idea of having to fake your way to the top felt so instinctively demeaning to me that I couldn't understand why anyone would want to make it that way.

Understand, in the neighborhoods of Brooklyn, there was no dreamy fantasizing about wanting to be a normal blue-eyed Protestant kid from a wholesome Midwestern family. In my neighborhood — Ocean Parkway, between Flatbush and Brighton Beach, sometimes called Gravesend — you could be Italian Catholic or Eastern European Jewish, period. When a Protestant kid showed up in school, once in a blue moon, having moved to Brooklyn from somewhere out there where the buffalo roam, we thought he was freaky. We liked our pizza and spumoni, our chicken soup and chopped liver, and had no desire to trade it in. James Johnson, whose family did, was considered a bit freaky, too, especially because there didn't even seem to be any payoff for the trade-off — he was no materially better off than we were, was in fact in the bottom to middle level, since he was apartment bound, and many of us were row housed.

John Waterman was a Protestant genie locked in a black phone. No combination of exchanges, neither Murray Hill nor Gramercy, Dewey, or Esplanade with any combination of numbers trailing would set him free. And even though his phone had an aura of danger around it (what would happen, I sometimes wondered, if I screwed up, answered the Waterman phone with "Comet Travel," or "Leo Lazar's office"? Would it bring the feds in, some square and threatening G-men come to arrest my father for impersonating a Protestant, which I imagined to be a felony?), it was mostly a magical object of fun. My father certainly had the knack of doing the voices of other regions and nationalities, and I picked it up. There's a thrill in impersonation that I still get a kick out of. Though I've progressed a bit beyond Sir Walter Raleigh in a can, I do enjoy leaving enigmatic phone messages for friends in voices impossible to identify. I don't get tickets to the game for this, but one takes one's amusement where one finds it. Where am I left, having circled around the story of a phone and a name? Maybe with the question of entrée, of using what the culture gives us by the back door when the front door seems unavailable, a large No Solicitation sign.

My father has told this story many times: he was a staff sergeant, was stationed in Calcutta, having dinner at the mess. Leo used to wax lyrically disgusted about the torments of army food. About Spam. He left his plate half-full (half-empty?), and a passing lieutenant ordered him to *clean it*. He refused, was reported, performed the requisite KP, and never advanced further in rank. *Anything further, Father?*

There are things we refuse, turn down, turn away from — bigger houses out of the ethnic soup of Brooklyn, for example, or women in Tennessee with yellow hair, who almost seem to shine with a shiksa brightness, or the grail of a diploma of higher learning. And there are things we end-run around, for compensation, for a sense of efficacy, for love of family and opportunity.

In 1972, I went to see Groucho Marx at Carnegie Hall. It was one of the hottest tickets ever in New York, a legendary swan song: just Groucho onstage, with young Marvin Hamlisch providing accompaniment at the piano. There were stories, jokes, bits of songs: "Lydia the Tattooed Lady," "It's Better to Go to Toronto, Than Live in a Place

You Don't Vant to." I got there early, went with my best friend. I can't remember ever being more excited about a performance. My brother and I knew virtually every Marx Brothers routine by heart. We'd riff off them for hours. This is so simple a four-year-old child could understand it. Somebody run and get me a four-year-old child. Or, to Margaret Dumont: Meet me tonight under the moon. You wear a tie so I'll know it's you. Or the speakeasy scene from *Horsefeathers*. Chico: I give you three guesses. It's the name of a fish. Groucho: Is it Mary? Chico: That's-a no fish. Groucho: Oh, yeah, she drinks like one. My friend and I cruised around Carnegie Hall, talked to Dick Cavett for a while, hoisted him up onstage at one point. The crowd started drifting in. In a burst of chutzpah, I went over to Mayor Lindsay, who was seated with his wife, and asked if he was going to drop out of the presidential race so that he wouldn't hurt McGovern's chances. In gentlemanly fashion, he said he hadn't decided yet, but was glad to see a young man so engaged with politics. I snagged autographs from some of my favorites (including Lindsay!): Jules Feiffer, Paul Simon and Art Garfunkel, Woody Allen, and just to round out the list, Chuck McCann, the sometime character actor and children's-show host famous for his manic readings, in costume, of Little Orphan Annie. It was a heady night, the crowd packed with celebrities.

I sat in the fourth row center, waiting for the next wave of wisecracks from the pantheon, the Ur-wit, Minnie's boy become a legend. John Waterman got me the tickets, in a move I vaguely remember as especially daring. Maybe he was deputy director of the United Jewish Appeal, or perhaps the grand duke of Freedonia. In any case, I remain grateful.

Movies Are a Mother to Me

apologies to Loudon Wainwright III

Did he have a mother? . . . How many people are sepulchred in us?
— *Edward Dahlberg*, Because I Was Flesh

t's a hot summer afternoon in Brooklyn, circa 1965, and my mother and I have just been to the hardware store, Doody's, which never failed to charm me both with its variety of products — everything from lumber and appliances, to hinges, tools, small metal whatchamacallits that seemed to have some astonishingly esoteric uses — and of course for its excremental name. The latter usually took center stage when my brother and I were in the car; it required fraternal goofiness; otherwise, it was too familiar for a titter, much like that other absurd name of my youth: Stephen Lipshitz, the hunchback of David A. Boody Junior High. These names, I might add, along with that of my least favorite uncle — Hyman Pergament — have always seemed to me near the top of the "You know names *can* be changed" scale. Before I slide into essayistic nominalism, let me tell you I liked the smell of wood, a dramatically clean tonic of a smell. And I liked hot hot days because they promised dramatic thunderstorms. I was a veritable little drama queen of the senses. I had my mother to myself this day. We returned from the hardware store and the air was as heavy as air gets — when it seems one is carrying it from place to place only to lay it on top of another heavy layer of air that one must carry someplace else, as though we were trying to build castles in the air with cinder blocks or were the grain to the air's millstone. I rolled down our porch awning, the creaky sound of metal and old dry fabric, as the sky darkened and then darkened some more. My mother was in the kitchen cooking Friday supper, and nothing could be wrong with chopped liver on its way. I remember the light

My mother is sometimes a movie to me.

inside the kitchen as orangy. I kept turning back and forth from the dark day, thunder just starting its distant warning, to my mother and her quiet bustle. Once she caught my eye and turned away. The thunder came closer. And then it all burst apart. The sky flashed on the dark day as if a cosmic light switch were clicking on and off, and rain came down in sheets for five minutes. Memory, you know; it might have been seven. And they might have been buckets. I might have been seven or eleven — memory's roll of the dice. The rain stopped but the day stayed dark, and the sidewalks steamed, and the only thing that hadn't changed was the orange light with my mother moving inside it. I think about this memory frequently before I go to sleep, I run it as a memory film, as if to tell myself that everything's okay, to give myself the lie that rescued moments are reclaimed, though I know that, in the words of James Agee, they cannot ever tell me who I am.

Faye Dunaway's slow, convulsive death at the end of Arthur Penn's *Bonnie and Clyde*— as though petit mort were the sound machine-guns make — has haunted me for thirty-five years. I walked out of a summer matinee, a bit excited and sad because of the slow-mo shoot-em-up ending. I wanted Bonnie and Clyde to live, and I thought, in my eleven-year-old way, that this violent scene was inexpressibly sad, and pretty neat, thoughts to that effect. I was waiting for my mother to pick me up. And I was sure that I wasn't sure how I could tell her this and be allowed to go to this kind of movie again. Some part of me was urging me not to say a word. I always had a habit of telling my mother things that I later became embarrassed about. As when I admitted that Honor Blackman was more beautiful than she after I saw *Goldfinger* and fell in love with Pussy Galore. I thought I needed to be honest since it was always our mother-son mantra, something like call and response, that she was the most beautiful woman in the world. This queasy relationship to intimacy continues in my life. I'm always telling people things that allow them to know me better and immediately regretting it if the response isn't convulsively embracing. I remember, abashedly, telling my mother when I had my first wet dream when I was twelve. She was really very nice about it for someone who was clearly flummoxed by my unexpected revelation. My relationship with my mother eventually turned "flummox" into a psychoanalytic category all its own, something combining oedipus and mawkishness, guilt and love so intertwined it can only be called "glove." She turned away, but she always turned away so gracefully that my problem with my self-giveaways never resolved, as though in turning away, I, her long-lost memorialist, am perpetually turning into a column of salt, mining her and myself into a quarry of lifelong digressions. Or is it a quandary? As William Hazlitt says in "The Fight," "Where was I?"

My mother took me to see *A Clockwork Orange* when it came out. It was playing in a theater on the Upper East Side of Manhattan, and we had long done summer outings for shopping/lunch/movies centered around Bloomingdale's and Alexander's and the movie theaters on Third Avenue. My mother had good, middle-class taste in art, which I say without a shred of condescension. My parents were always willing to take us to see some new controversial play that they thought would stimulate thought and discussion. It's the part of the middle class that I love — the idea of families willing to stretch themselves a bit, let themselves think about some things outside the usual purview. And my parents — neither of whom were college educated, while both were sharp and funny, and my father with a worldly philosophical streak — were devotees of the idea of Culture, especially where their children were concerned. We walked out of the movie theater on Third Avenue, and my mother seemed a bit amused that she had taken her thirteen-year-old son to see the film — not regretful, mind you, but . . . bemused. I remember my mother saying that the film "had a lot going on." I think I said, "No kidding," and something about never having seen a world like that in the movies (I wouldn't call them films for another two or three years, and then with the lump of pretension in my throat, at least until late graduate school). We drove home to Brooklyn rather silently, each of us in some space between groovy ultraviolence and the uneasy and euphoric feeling (here's where I do the Faye Dunaway Chinatown scene — uneasy, euphoric, uneasy, euphoric) that mother and son had had a rather strangely intense experience.

In 1973 I went by myself to see Buñuel's *Discrete Charm of the Bourgeoisie* at the Waverly, on Sixth Avenue. I told my mother I was going to see Buñuel, and she asked me if he was a new boy at school. I said he was a director, and she laughed at herself genially — not a central characteristic of Buñuel's bourgeoisie. At the end of the film, a little dog went running up the aisle, and I thought, *Of course, at the end of a Buñuel film a dog should run up the aisle. Un chien perdu?* I told my mother about the dog, and she asked me what kind it was. My mother always asked what I thought were ridiculous questions that I hadn't considered. I had no idea, of course, because I just kept thinking, pretentiously, yes, a dog and Buñuel, isn't that just perfect?

For my second date with Wendy Takahisa (my first had been to see Bob Dylan at Madison Square Garden on my seventeenth birthday), we planned to go see Zeffirelli's *Romeo and Juliet*. Yes, yes, isn't that adorable. But I was sick as a dog. Which I suppose means that I was as sick as a sick dog, which I suppose means I was quite sick, in the dog days of a bad cold. But I suppose it was a measure of my extreme self-confidence that I thought it crucial that I go through with it, that if I didn't it would put the kibosh on any building or budding dating momentum. I loaded up on cold medicine, and off we went, bus to bus to movie theater on Kings Highway. I put my elbow on the seat rest and leaned my head against my palm. And slept through just about everything other than the credits, slept like a sick cat, though I think a sickly version of the theme song, "A Time for Us," wafted surreally across my consciousness for two hours. It strikes me that this is the only memory I have in which I was sick cats and dogs. We went home, awkwardly said good-bye, and I spent every waking and many dreaming hours obsessing over when I might deign to attempt to kiss her and whether her second-date memory would inscribe me permanently as germ filled. My mother was waiting up for me, remarkably, since it was way past nine when I returned; my parents started makwing preparations for bed at around six A.M. "How was the movie?" "It was, you know, *Romeo and Juliet*. Olivia Hussey was a really cute Juliet (shouldn't have said that)." My mother's endgame: "Was it worth going out with a girl when you're this sick?" A shrug, but my thought: definitively: of course, without question, to be with a girl at any given time or circumstance of life? Of course. I said nothing, but my mother had already turned to go to into the bedroom, not quite as gracefully or acceptingly this time.

One winter, when I was eighteen or nineteen, home from college for a long break, I went walking in a Brooklyn snow in the early morning. The streets were lovely, dark, and deep. Another solitary figure was out walking, directly toward me, and I wondered, Notes from the Underground–like, who would yield the snow path first. The question obliterated at twenty paces when I realized I was heading for Gavrielle Gleich, on whom I had a grand crush in high school. Gavrielle Gleich, what an unlikely name for a young man's muse — she inspired me to write, and I was continually creating movie scenarios that would lead to a linked fate: a foggy meeting on Waterloo Bridge, with the Brooklyn Bridge substituted; waiting for her on top of the Empire State Building — the observation deck à la *An Affair to Remember*, not King Kong and Faye Wray — only to realize, years later, that she hadn't ditched me (not ditched but a glitch with Gleich; it sounds like a Dr. Seuss romantic fantasy — something along the lines of Horton Has a Honey, or The Gleitch Who Stole Christmas). To think that for several years my frenzied erotic fantasies circled around Gleich. Yikes; it sounds, somehow, untidy. Gav was pretty in a plain way that I always felt was prettier than pretty, and quite bright, verbally witty. She was the only person in my high school who I felt was potentially smarter than I. She had a smirk that was pure and worldly — it said something like "I've seen it all, and I'm still not jaded" — and I was constantly trying to impress her, to see if I could register something new on those lips. *And and and* had I been a guest on *You Bet Your Life*, I would have gamely jousted with Groucho just to see a duck descend with her name. There she was, trudging toward me in the snow on Ocean Parkway, nobody else around. We smiled at each other and immediately started walking in a direction neither of us had been headed toward, a kind of pedestrian pas de deux. I remember that at one point we sang Paul Simon's "I Am a Rock" in harmony: "A winter's day, in a deep and dark December" — one of us started singing, she, most likely, and the other just joined in. We sat down on a snowy apartment stoop on some side block and talked for a while. And I suggested we go to my house to hang out. She agreed, and I was immediately seized by the kind of panic that had always accompanied my slide from fantasy into possibility. This would last for years to come; yearning and panic, yearning and panic, my neuroses a geometric pattern repeating themselves like an Escher painting, and frequently even less interesting.

When we got to my house, I reintroduced her to my mother, and we headed downstairs, and I could tell my mother was not at all a happy . . . mother. She must have smelled some young hormone of horniness steaming off the top of my head like snow melting in a dramatic thaw. We went downstairs anyhow.

In my room, my little, brown shag–carpeted, wood-paneled enclave, *grotto* might actually capture it more closely, Gav came up with the idea of our not speaking a word, but having a conversation through writing, writing a screenplay that was the documentary of our contemporaneous interaction. After my head stopped spinning like a gynoscope — sorry, make that gyroscope — I was both tantalized — since writing my desires seemed easier than speaking them — and scared, since I had even less of an excuse to avoid making my desires known than my usual strategy of delaying sexual initiations until I could further delay sexual initiations until some mundane machina threw a wrench in to scotch any chance at all, which is conventionally known, via Pascal I believe, as the dilemma of the chance-scotching wrench. Nothing happened, other than a lot of sexual tension. I still have the pages buried somewhere; years ago I looked at them and marveled at my pathetic brinksmanship — always on the brink of saying . . . something, and always keeping it completely implicit. Eventually, my mother called downstairs one time too many to ask me some inconsequential question, and Gav decided it was time to go. The movie flickered and stopped, the characters we were playing, versions of ourselves, suddenly stood awkwardly on camera with their mouths open and nothing coming out. I ran into her once a couple of years later. She was, I seem to remember, working as a laborer, but planning to get married to an Englishman and move to Suffolk or Essex, but it was all Norfolk to me. I marveled that she had started to look like a minilinebacker, but had this romantically exotic future ahead of her. It was as though Lady Caroline Lamb had been grafted onto Eugene V. Debs.

In my mind's movie, my mother is still long-dead, but occasionally my old Gav-script gets played out to feature length, except that we're both unnaturally young, the snow is perennially pure Vermont white (as opposed to Brooklyn off-white), a Gleitch-muse makes perfect sense, and it all ends without a hitch.

We had one clunky old air conditioner in our row house, and it was in my parents' bedroom. On hot summer nights my brother and I would drag our mattresses in and lay them on the floor next to our parents' trundle bed. There we were, the five of us (including our toy fox terrier, nicknamed Pig-dog by my brother because of her ungainly girth, developed by the fact that my mother would roast a chicken every week strictly for her) in a little room, with a nineteen-inch black-and-white TV, and cool air blowing over our heads by the shuddering, gasping, exaggeratedly named Frigidaire. It was an adventure; we were Robinson Crusoes, adrift in a cool bubble on a hot sea. I loved it the way kids love the normal routine busted up; it stops time, puts you in that familial state which is pure harmony inspired by novelty. It was on that night that I watched *The Man Who Shot Liberty Valence* for the first time. My parents were indifferent, I believe — never big John Wayne or western fans. But I was experiencing some rather complex emotions. Wayne was incredibly familiar to my seven- or eight-year-old self, of course, but mostly through the mostly cheesy films he was making in the midsixties. But here he was, and I was finding him irresistible. I think I was a bit thrown off by Jimmy Stewart, at the age of fifty-five or so, playing a young law graduate and wearing an apron and getting kicked around. It seemed weird that an older man would be getting treated like such a pansy — weren't bullies reserved for kids only? But John Wayne said Liberty Valence was "the toughest man south of the Picket Wire, 'cept for me," and I thought that if I was ever that tough I wanted to be just that casually confident about it. I still would, in the unlikely event that I ever have the chance. I somehow can't see myself saying, "Liberty Valence is the best essayist north of the Ohio River, 'cept for me." Though I kind of like the idea. The other line that rang and rings was when Wayne told Stewart, "You didn't shoot Liberty Valence," the fact that makes this, of all things, a John Ford revisionist western. The truth was therefore elusive — I got the point.

In the morning the heat had broken, and my brother and I went back to the banal exile of our room next door. For weeks my mother had to endure my tacking on "'cept for me" at the end of every sentence. Things like "Everybody thinks that Richie is this great guy, 'cept for me." John Wayne became even more of an appalling figure as I aged into political consciousness later in the sixties. Still, at the back of my mind, there was this unshakably appealing swagger tinged with bitterness inspired by a crowded night in a cool little room. No one seems to remember that night, 'cept for me.

We used to go to Radio City Music Hall to see a movie on Christmas day, my brother's birthday. These were the years, in the sixties, when Radio City was well into the process of acquiring the look of faded grandeur, which I always hate to see replaced by ornate restoration. I know that this is a somewhat perverse attitude, but I stand by it. It's the same reasoning collectors use for preferring a marked-up and untouched original to a repainted, refinished, or reconstructed version. Who with any shred of taste really prefers the work of cosmetic surgery, no matter how civicly sensible. The movies we saw were mostly big clunkers: *Ice Station Zebra*, for example. We suffered through these, then dined and drove home. One Christmas, on the Gawannis Parkway, with my mother at the wheel, and my brother and I *drimmelling* (Yiddish for going in and out of sleep) in the backseat, the car in front of my mother hit a big dog (very strange and improbable on the elevated highway). I felt the car jerk and swerve and sat up to see the dog spinning in smooth circles on the road as we drove past. When we got home, my mother lavished attention on our little Pig-dog. My mother then poured herself an extremely rare glass of Harvey's Bristol Cream, and I headed for bed, only to dream, in one of my most memorable childhood dreams, that Mom was a Rockette, and I was older, sitting in the audience, and judging the dancers for something important.

My brother and I had been positively salivating about seeing *2001: A Space Odyssey*. My mother took us to the city to see it on the day it opened. We braved a long line and got in. I remember having a soft spot for Hal and wanting him to live and be rehabilitated, and a long stream of people walking quietly down the street after the film. The only discussion I recall is that my brother, my mother, and I exchanged brief, mystified articulations about what the famous sequence at the end was all about. I felt I wanted to really like the film, and was terribly confused and a little afraid of my inability to articulate what the sequence meant, the return to embryonic psychedelia. I didn't like that one bit, and was frustrated and sad that my mother did this great thing in taking us and that I couldn't say I really really loved the movie, because I hadn't understood it.

I used the movies to fantastically supplement all of my relationships. My family romance was completely cinematic. My brother was Lew Ayres in *Holiday*, my father Lewis Stone or Boris Karloff, my mother Ethel Barrymore or late Katharine Hepburn, my imaginary sister Judy Garland or Myrna Loy, my girlfriend Jeanne Moreau, Carole Lombard, Margaret Sullivan . . . my best friend Edmund O'Brien or Bogart or John Garfield. There were countless variations on these themes. I, of course, was always myself, but glorified by courage, glamorized by wit, lionized for steadfastness of unpopular but utterly righteous belief, and beautifully slender like Leslie Howard. Ah, if I'd only had a brain, a heart, da nerve. I was the best part of every great celluloid human moment I had ever seen, without question, without fail, and without curfew.

I love looking at pictures of my mother between the ages of seventeen and twenty-five. Her clothes in the high school pictures, all in black and white, were forties-impeccable: alpaca coats, bobby socks, mary janes, white cotton blouses without too much starch. For some reason, almost all of the photos I have (as the archivist for my family) are autumn photos — a coincidental seasoning of my photographic past. Certainly my grandfather — a master tailor who managed to look natty and dignified in a bathing suit — would have sanctioned my mother's attention to crisp and fashionable wear. Like my grandfather, her outfits are always handsome, but with just a hint of special care for fashion. Amazing the way good fabrics communicate their quality photographically.

In the early fifties, as a young married woman, she blooms into a kind of iconic figure, photographically, as though the movies were being copied with a kind of careless alacrity. Her young body seems to hum in a gold lamé evening gown, a black dinner dress accented by a languid cigarette-savvy wrist. My father always looks stunned by a sense of good fortune. Overall, I'm always amazed at how many old black-and-white photos look exactly like movie stills, but insisting on this may, in dreams, begin irresponsibility.

My parents would watch old movies as they went to sleep. In the next room, a thin wall separating us, I would shout good-nights and catch phrases, which my mother would have to answer in sequence. This must have occurred between the ages of six and eight, Dr. Watson, since from eight, when my grandmother downstairs was widowed, until eleven, when she became quite ill, my brother and I took turns staying the night with her, sleeping in the same bed in what seems to me now an almost unbearably sweet nod back to the Ukranian shtetls. Or a confused New World understanding of bundling. And I always remember my brother in the room and his mocking consternation when my mother and I were shouting our catechism, his Wicked Witch of the West imitations of me, as though I were shouting "Auntie Em, Auntie Em" to the next room. My father would lose his temper sometimes and scream to me to be quiet and go to sleep, at which point all of us, including my father, would start into a kind of freeze-framed stillness. Such a mama's boy . . . I'd weep into my pillow and the sound of the movie on the old Philco would filter through the wall as the replacement for my mother's voice.

My mother's complexities are all oblique or circumstantial to me now, as though her character, her "herness" were a mere subtext to twenty years of maternal hermeneutics. Part of the reason I'm compelled to write about her is, no doubt, because of a feeling that while I was very close to her, that while I can remember the timbre of her voice (if a voice falls in a forest and someone hears it . . .), I feel retrospectively that either I was immune to knowing her in a complicated way — no, I have always known her in a complicated way, just haven't had her available to the adult me — or that she wasn't really all that complicated, an idea that would leave me swimming upstream, trying to solve the red herring of parental mystery, which I believe is a triple mixed metaphor. It's not as though this takes the shine off her memory — far from it; I demand complexity from my friends, but have always preferred (usually unsuccessfully) simplicity from my family. If I were to film my mother's life, the camera would have to linger, waiting for her face itself to say something that sheds light. Or the film would be about a distraught son who sometimes confuses metaphysics with slapstick. But the audience might not find him risible, though he might so find himself. If when I write about my mother, my focus on myself seems narcissistic, it's because I'm the only route to her I know. If we really want to know D. W. Griffith, perhaps we have to focus on Lillian Gish, trying desperately not to get swept away — call it the *Orphans of the Storm* approach to biography.

When I go to a movie, I'm in a kind of daze in my seat before the lights even lower. It's a kind of focused somnabulence, a dazed passivity with just a quiver of anticipation thrown in. I don't like to talk at all once I hit my seat, and have to resist the urge to tell others to be quiet even before the previews begin. Shush, please, the film will be starting in five minutes. My heartbeat settles to a slower rhythm, but I feel, vaguely, like I'm waiting for the visual abreaction that will settle everything once and for all, meaning once and for me. I don't like to be touched in the movies, and even eating popcorn takes on a kind of rhythmically repetitive, almost masturbatory edge. Time seems hushed and heavy — the six minutes before the screen fills with light usually feel like hours, like little lifetimes, except womblike, inchoate. As I've aged, the experience of the films themselves have become almost inevitably disappointing. But, hey, so is the movement out of the womb. You think you're about to take off, and all you get is the same old tired slap, with maybe a flying dream down the road. These days, too often,

I feel like the movies don't give me enough. Ten minutes in, and I'm bored — the rhapsody chased right out of me, despite my almost endless goodwill. It isn't that I could ever stop going, though, or commute the feeling that I'm about to be told something startling, ushered into some visually sea-changed space where the answers to questions I didn't know I had fill up the screen like a Jenny Holzer aphorism speeding across my forehead. And perhaps that is (my hyped-up fingers just typed *id*, and, to paraphrase Bill Clinton, I guess it all depends upon what *id* is) what happens when I think of my mother: I get this flickering light that signals the start of the film, but then I have to project the images myself — no real answers, but after all, better than nothing at all.

On Three Fraternal Aphorisms

A sibling is a cracked mirror of identity.
In memories begin responsibilities.
Autobiographical essays are always epistolary.

riting aphorisms is a dangerous game: you'd better
be interesting and pithy, or you lose credibility, badly.
So, I may be throwing down three gauntlets (which
I've always thought sounded like undernourished
children) by beginning with them.

A sibling is a cracked mirror of identity. But unlike Patty Duke and her cousin, Cathy, my brother
and I do not walk alike, although at times we do talk alike. Scott's walk
is a bit ducky — there's a touch of waddle in it. I walk, as I do most
things, with a painfully acquired self-consciousness. I walk with a kind
of girlish swagger, as though the other girls on the stoop are watching
me approach a guy and I want to show how really confident I am. My
walk isn't completely girlish, though, because I learned from years of
living in cities that the way I walk would project whether or not I were
a good target for 1) robbing, 2) thrashing about the face and neck,
3) verbal abuse of this sort: Take that, you girlish walker!

So I mixed some "guy" in with my perambulating style. I realize I
now sound as though I parade about with a bit of licorice hanging
from my mouth and a come-hither look in my eye, but really I think I
walk rather wittily. That's it; I walk as though I were about to say something pithy and amusing, as though I were about to commit, say, an
aphorism. My walk puts a certain amount of pressure on me, creates
anticipation. If I weren't sitting here writing (writers are always sitting
ducks), I'd change it immediately.

Scott's walk, previously identified as mallardly — though Bugs
Bunny wouldn't be too far off, either — is unobjectionable, but not

uninteresting. The presence of a bit of behind in his walk belies his speed, and the friendliness of his approach when he's not in a rush. My brother will amble up to you if he likes you. His intentions are in his walk, as opposed to being announced by them, as in my case. In that sense, his walk seems, is, unaffected. I remember playing basketball with Scott when we were teenagers and into our twenties, and always being surprised by his speed. We're both small, and I was rather fast after I lost my teenage weight, but Scott was just as fast or faster. He's average weight, had been on the slim side of average when younger, but that bit of a duck ass looked like he couldn't move very quickly. But he has enormous determination when he's focused, and his speedometer shows off the effort, and he becomes the little engine that can. When he's angry, he walks like a tense duck in midtempo, his anger seeming to fuel the movement, a mechanical duck. He swims the same way: hard, chopping little strokes that you think can't possibly be making him move so well.

I swim in long elegant strokes. I can do about a lap before petering out.

When I'm angry, I slow myself down, afraid of my beating heart, the pounding in my ears. I feel like I'm floating, and I think I look like someone who is ill and trying to find a solitary space without showing the need for it.

When I'm happy to see someone, I, too, amble up, perhaps a bit seductively.

Scott's friends look happy to see him because of who he is. Mine, I worry, look happy to see me because of what I might say. This sounds rather insecure; I'll leave it to my friends to convince me otherwise.

To return to Patty Duke — yes, yes, he says in a feint of a faint on the chaise, one must always return to Patty Duke — Scott and I do not look alike to most people. I look like Anyeuropean (English, with a dash of the Balkans, and just a hint of Lichtenstein), which has always suited my desire for constant incognito. I think I can see some of my mother's Russian Jewish parents, but the wideness of their faces is absent. They were wide-faced, my father's side Jewish Roman-nosed; they apparently fought to a draw in me.

Scott is straight Leo, fully paternal in his facial inheritance. He's much handsomer than he knows, sometimes looking like a little

DeNiro. For years he would introduce me as "the one who got the looks," which sounds, presciently, like the one who got away. I always felt, embarrassedly, that the implication was that I didn't look Jewish. Yet I'm sure he didn't mean that consciously.

Nevertheless, when I look at Scott, I see a version of my eyes, a slightly paler green perhaps. And my light brown hair, though I was curlier younger and have straightened out, and he's wavier now. Our arms and legs and ears are similar — as though a demented doll-maker prayed to the god of the sum of the parts.

Most everyone thinks we look little alike, aside from the occasional malcontent who insists, perversely, on the intense similarity. The point is not what the world sees when they line us up, but what we see when we look eye to eye. I see a memory of two adolescent bodies walking home from Sheepshead Bay, when we pass the adult me staring too intently at the two of us. We shake our heads and make a wisecrack or two, and continue walking home together — occasionally brushing against each other — what must such almost-registered pleasures have been like? — stopping to buy thick vanilla shakes on a hot bright afternoon in Brooklyn, thirty or forty years ago.

Scott stayed in New York, stayed committed to his life as a family man, working a profession he's good at but doesn't care very much about. This sounds like I'm moving into riddle: it pays well, but requires long hours; you use your brain, but there's plenty of paperwork; we all need it, but we don't all use it. And your walk is only important when you stride into a courtroom. Oh, darn! Class, I'm so sorry: I gave it away.

Our sibling model is familiar: the elder goes the more practical route: lawyering, close to home, early marriage; the younger, the less conventional direction: wandering off in the graduate school wilderness in a less practical search for poetry and love. I seemed to have inherited the travel agency, domestically: I haven't lived near my family for twenty-five years. Because we were too close and not close enough? In all families someone performs the Unnamable: we can't move on, we can move on, we move on.

"At least you're doing what you love, David," says the lawyer.

"I don't love teaching freshman composition classes," says the graduate student.

"At least you've got a family, Scott," says the graduate student. "It's exhausting having two kids and a job you don't love," says the lawyer.

We jousted and commiserated through the years of early adulthood, but the difference came down to this: He got New York; I got literature. That's probably an even trade on many levels. I wouldn't trade poetry and essays even for Brooklyn, which almost breaks my heart to say; but here I choose to stay.

But, you say, tapping your fingers impatiently on the table: what about Scott, your brother?

Yes: Scott is extremely reflective when he's not angry. His mind is fiercely incisive; but he hasn't read very much of any importance in the last twenty-five years; who could, with job and kids and kids' extracurricular stuff and trying to stay active in the Jewish Community Center? Reading when you're exhausted at ten o'clock at night requires ubermenschian discipline. You can tell he wants to have been reading books and it makes him unhappy in a nervous sort of way that he hasn't, since he keeps up with the culture in most other ways: movies, theater, music, sports. This is probably why he idealizes the profession of professing: it's my job to do what he can't find the time for, and would love. His intellect has been overcommitted to lawyering, which is too narrow for Scott's intellectually epicurean curiosity.

I've asked my brother what his fantasy job is. His response: film critic. And I can see it: he's at a desk at the Times building (he's smarter, after all, than most of the *Times* film critics) rendering passionate judgments. When we talk, instead of our usual litany of things seen and done, he sparks out glittering pieces of cinematic detritus that make me say "No!" and "Really? Not really!?" such as, "Did you know that Jeanne Moreau was really a man? That Orson Welles was really nine when he made *Citizen Kane*? That Nosferatu was played by a young Tab Hunter?" Except, you know, they would be true. Perhaps Scott's fantasy self is close to my fantasy brother — but I fear that means more like me, and I hesitate to wish that on anyone, even myself. I divulge the fantasy with a bit of a gulp, a gulp preceding this statement: Scott and I are close/not close. Or: do we feel closer than we are? Here I turn to you to ask you to stop a moment to consider whether you have a version of this kind of relationship, the kind that, when people ask whether or not you're close, you stumble, you fudge it a bit. You aren't quite sure, though you may have known this person since he first peeled the lead paint off his windowsill waiting for you to be brought home into the world. Though if he needed any-thing — money, advice, an essay — I'd give it to him almost without hesitation.

Closeness is a feeling that doesn't even seem certifiable as a feeling. Is saying "I feel close," rather than "I am close," a way of noting how incomplete or fragile our relational distinctions can be? And maybe that speaks most pertinently to my own fraternal drama. I can't be ac-cused of fraternizing too often with my brother. I see him, these days, once a year, once every two years. We talk every couple of months or so. How's the kids? What have you seen? Damn Knicks! Damn Yan-kees! Damn Republicans!

Perhaps we're too much alike to not feel close, but not enough alike to be closer.

A sibling is a cracked mirror of identity.

I got him a little drunk on scotch when my son was born a couple of years ago; we drank Dalmore to Delmore, then ventured into more dangerous territories about how our family made us who we are, a nar-rative filled with rivers of milk and bile. When he spoke about his insecurities, long-standing from his late teens, when his long march in academic excellence seemed to stumble along with his social life, I felt the kind of cracking open in sympathy one can only feel toward those one loves most deeply. I immediately felt — no, knew — that we needed time alone together every year.

I like to try to engage the people I love in grand gestures. Let's meet once a year for a weekend in some exotic place, I said. Okay, he said. He looked drunkenly dubious. Or I'll try to get a close friend to agree to a different ritual: this restaurant is so fabulous: let's all go here once a month, say the second Saturday of every month, forever. Or "Let's sit at the pond at sunset, always. Forever. Even after we're dead! Okay?" Perhaps my years of bachelorhood gave me a forlorn desire for ritual that now plays out in forlorn gestures of symbolic grandeur that deflate as I'm proposing them: Let's all . . . okay, let's you and me . . . we have to do this all the time. . . . But reality, indeed, frequently does bite back: I want to see my brother more; he wants to see me more. But we don't seem willing to do much about it. Let's do it always becomes let's think about it.

To return to my first aphorism. My brother and I have similar voices. But I lost most of my New York accent years ago on my tours around the country's halls of academe. Scott, a few years ago, became self-conscious about his New York accent, perhaps because of his kids; so he decided to change his *a*s. He now speaks with a New York accent in which every other *a* is pronounced with exaggerated Midwestern flatness. The result, if one is paying attention, is rather delightful, as though he knew a secret patois.

It is when we speak together that we sound most alike, when the words that most of the people in my world wouldn't understand (meeskite, meshugas, tsoris), or the neologisms and in-jokes that found their homes under the roofs of our family language years ago, emerge. Scott ratchets up his discourse a bit when he speaks to me, competing at times with his baby brother's Ph.D. I try to loosen up, not condescendingly, but to avoid sounding like an egghead. We meet somewhere in the middle, I think, sounding a bit alike, perhaps while discussing *The Patty Duke Show*.

Is my brother more Jewish than I? This has been the general family verdict. I think it's possible that I *feel* more Jewish. I long ago renounced belief in much besides Art, Love, and Social Justice. A bit of belief probably clings to my body; the brain is the easiest organ to wash of such things, once you put your mind to it. My brother goes to shule, bar- and bat-mitzvahs his kids; partakes of the community life of Jewish culture. I'm diasporic: I moved around the fringes of this country: California, Texas, upstate New York. To many people, I suppose, I'm not a Jew: no synagogue, no belief, no contributions to UJA. I've lived my life, though, with a sense of being marked, having the mark of David and Solomon, Leopold and Loeb, Julius and Ethel, on my forehead. I'm more Holocaust-haunted than Scott. In New York, in staying with the fold (he's a bit fuzzy on the actual matter of belief), my brother experiences his Jewishness as belonging, rather than separating, surrounded as he is by other belief-challenged practicing Jews.

Scott in Hebrew is Shlomo, Solomon. David is Dovid, David. We're the mythologized father/son reconfigured as siblings, so I'm older than my older brother — do you hear the logic of childhood arguments in this? My brother married very early on the heels of a light dating experience. I've been around the block a few too many times (set em up, Joe. . . .). Scott has a depth of family experience far beyond my own; I'm world-wearier and have taken poorer care of myself.

It must have required stupendous optimism to name two Jewish kids David and Solomon a few years after the Holocaust. The world mustn't know, though; too much of a mark, even in New York. So one became Scott, a goyish name par excellence. Scott is the kid in penny loafers whose father plays golf, and whose mother belongs to the DAR, no?

Scott managed to be more of a Jewish kid and more of a regular kid than I. He excelled at Hebrew School, was a straight A student. At sixteen, befitting the times, he had long, straightened hair, and my uncle Hymen called him Jesus Christ, which is more fun to say than it was for him to hear. Then he had a stranger, wavier haircut that I called the Aircraft Carrier. I, . . . well, he mostly fit in, while I seemed to be cut from different cloth. Fat, hopeless at Hebrew, phobic, a quirky, struggling honor student, romantically moony, moody, and bedeviled by Brooklyn's finest brats. My brother's childhood was happier than mine, I think.

Except. Leo Lazar was a tough one for an eldest son. Fathers with furious egos are generally so. My brother has many accomplishments, but the one thing he doesn't have (and neither do I, though it hurts me less) is an aura of being a sheer force of nature, which is one of my father's points of definition. My brother and I lack the energetic certainty that my father forged against small odds, like war and poverty. Scott has felt less powerful than Leo, whereas he is merely different, a son. I, feeling different early, suffered early, but less so later on.

There are jokes I share only with my brother. Many of these are familial; Scott relies on me to invoke pain comically, as a reminder that it is there. This might include references to our dead mother, other relatives (Uncle Ruby busted me for trying to see my grandmother in the hospital — I was too young by the hospital rules he suddenly became the agent of; or I might say to Scott, "Isn't it funny that all our cousins are named Gevalt?" — a Yiddish exclamatory sigh of a word); or I might mention Gravesend, our Brooklyn neighborhood (remember the mansion around the corner, on Manhattan Court, impossibly large and mysteriously removed from the rest of the street, surrounded by wrought-iron fences and large spruces; they replaced it with a few row houses — how was that possible, unless they shrank the property, unless someone has sabotaged our memories with enlargement?), or teachers we shared (Rabbi Schlomo's big ears, we called him Rabbi Dumbo; Mrs. Plisner calling me Scott for all of fifth grade, except when I corrected her, and she apologized as though I were interrupting with the trivial, my name), or occasions (going with him to my first Yankee game, the long ride from Brooklyn to the Bronx; I mutilated an advertising slogan on the walk back from the train station, singing, "It's the flavor that you favor when you need an amputator"; I was eight or so). Memories cut the difference and make us allies, secret sharers of a memory cell. Scott counts on me to be the rememberer, a role I've relished for as long . . .

Fraternizing with your brother in an autobiographical essay is like dancing a fractured pas de deux, a pas d'un. Are we close? At times I wish we needed each other more. Our need for each other is, I think, latent, and powerful. The idea of him not being in the world opens up the slough of despond for me, that bottomless, harmless-looking puddle on the corner of Ocean Parkway and Avenue X in Brooklyn, which holds, in its depths, our most intense feelings of loneliness, Jimmy Hoffa, something like guilt for not having spun each other closer in the webs of our lives, and Rhoda Lazar, our dead mother, floating like Shelly Winters in *Night of the Hunter* in a light, diaphanous dress that sheds light on the murky waters of our subconscious. My mother's death, when I was twenty-three and he twenty-five, is the trauma we've just been emerging from these last few years. And part of our dilemma, part of not coming to grips with how close we were or could be, was a sense that we couldn't fill the vacuum of intimacy that she left. As young men, or perhaps just as human grievers, we misunderstood the timeline of grief. Scott and I could have partially filled what felt to me like scarecrow hollow-heartedness, or haunted heartedness, after her death; the ghost of her . . . in our lost family romance ("there's a ghost of you within my haunted heart, ghost of you my lost romance. . . ."). We didn't know we could get closer, or how. I think I, for one, transfixed by pain, froze at times into fraternal inertia.

My brother drives like a maniac. His driving is a displaced sense of anger at the world. Its ideology: the rules of the road are clear except for your own exceptions. It's fine to cut someone else off if you have to, but it's never okay for someone to cut you off. . . . He won't like my saying this; he's a defensive driver about certain things.

Scott goes to the theater all the time. And Knicks games. I get a twinge when I think of all of those years of Broadway he's had while I've been out in the repertory wilderness in Ohio (hold your letters, please). In 1962, when I was five and he eight, we sat next to each other at *Oliver*, our first show. We had front-row seats. The family repe-story (a repeated anecdote that has lost any direct connection to fact) has me openmouthed, enthralled, in love with the actress Georgia Brown. That is a darling image. We sat next to each other through hundreds of plays in the sixties and seventies: *Fiddler on the Roof* to *Sunday in the Park with George* (we were the house of Sondheim), Nicole Williamson in *Hamlet* and Dustin Hoffman in *Jimmy Shine*. But a kind of iterative memory jumps to the front of the line when I think of these years: the two of us trying not to laugh during some moment of intense drama.

We had been to dinner, always. Maybe even had a touch of wine from our parents' glasses. Perhaps we were logy, not theater-perky. As though on cue, during, say, *Merchant of Venice*, or *Equus* (Scott and I finding our way to the Old Vic, since the folks could get only two tickets . . . Alec McGowan, ahh), some grande dame sitting in front of us, coiffed — or let's say a Wall Street philistine who thought that going to the theater was something that one did, sitting in heavy gray flannel, tie too tight, perhaps drowsing through the first two acts — would inevitably, let's say at "Hath not a Jew . . . ," fart. It would probably be a squeak rather than a Gideon trumpet, a sound close enough to a seat moving, or perhaps a moving seat performing an act of mimicry in defiance of a life of sedation. Wooozeeeert. The breath of one of us would jam in furious resistance to laughter, which engaged the same mechanism in the other. We'd attempt to cough away the laugh, and a bizarre noise would emerge that at least released the tension temporarily. This experience may be the heart of siblinghood, and I'm sure you have your version of it. Ours was on Broadway in the sixties; mine was with Scott.

I've been able to make him laugh for almost as long as I can remember. This became my prerogative. Taking pleasure in making him laugh has helped make me who I am. I learned to be "wicked" early on, in the way the British use it — daringly bad, not purposelessly bad, and mostly verbally so. I learned, through Scott, to be shockingly funny. There is a lovely little space between bad taste and blunt honesty . . . that I would violate repeatedly. I might say that a certain uncle looked more like a carbuncle. Or I might lean and in a whisper ask, during a Seder dinner, if he had been thinking of oral sex during the Haggadah. To the extent that I enjoy shocking a bit, or saying the thing that I sense those around me want to say, but are afraid to, I owe a dedicated debt to Scott. There is a relationship between the reader of this book and my brother; you're both listening to me; I care what you think; I need your reactions, even if I need to imagine them as the reactions I need.

Scott can't tell jokes. When he does, he frequently tells them so badly that the fractured narrative supersedes the punch line, becomes the punch line. I remember times when he would start telling a joke and we would be in stitches by his stops and starts: "No, wait, a rabbi goes into a laundromat. No, I mean, he's working at a laudromat. No, at the luncheonette . . ." And I would participate by performing an anti-Socratic method. "What kind of a laundromat? Is my Aunt Minnie working there, too?"

Scott puns a lot. Puns always flew furiously in my family; it was the competitive sport we took most seriously. His own verbal dexterity has focused on the pun since we were kids. Sometimes he's sharp, and sometimes he's corny. He likes to use the lines we used when we were kids: Groucho lines, neighborhood lines, family lines, and I like to hear him say them. At times it's maddening to be around the two of us, or the three of us, on the rare occasions we're together with our father (Our father, who art in Delray, blessed be thy mane — that's how it might start). He smiles slyly, self-satisfied in a way that's rather endearing, after he gets one off, as though any attempt to one-up him would be a crime, irrelevant, that the reward of a groan should be his due. Sometimes I resist the impulse. I'll say, "Aren't we clever," and give him a bear hug. Sometimes now I can free myself of my compulsion to always, to always ejaculate. (I've made Scott laugh. . . .) It is the pleasure of speaking that frequently unites Scott and me — and that largely defines us: a kind of Freudian freude, including schadenfreude. We have two essential kinds of conversations on the phone: dull catch-ups, and free-for-all-punning carnivals.

There was so much laughter and so much anger in my family. Still, today, my brother, my father, and I are usually laughing with someone, making someone laugh, or burnishing our anger at the world or each other. Anger is an issue among the troika of father and sons. I'm almost incapable of expressing anger at my father. My brother does it passive-aggressively. My father's anger can come and go these days, like a tropical rain, not the monsoons of our youth.

One day when we were driving around England together in 1975, I eighteen and he twenty-one, Scott starting pummeling me as we were about to get on the M3, pounding my arm and chest, a rather dangerous game for the passenger in a car going seventy or so. I had made him that angry. On the same trip, we were so angry at each other that we decided to go separate ways for the day. I think we were in York, because I have a vague memory of an indistinct contrast to the heat we were producing, and Northern England makes some cool sense. I had left my wallet out in our B & B, and he had taken all my money. I was at sea for the day. I had a paperback with me, Larkin's *A Girl in Winter*, and I spent much of the day reading in the cathedral in a spot where light peeked through the doors in a shaft you could read by, if you found a well-placed seat. I don't remember what we had argued about, or how we reconciled. One more: I went to JFK airport to meet Scott and my father returning from a trip together. I was sixteen, I think, Scott therefore nineteen. My father got into a verbal altercation with some other curbside passengers. We were all waiting for "limos," taxis really; my father had had someone send one to pick us up (someone was almost always doing something for us because my father was almost always doing something for someone). There at the curb the dispute turned from whose cab it was, rather easily established, to the fact that my father was, according to these other folks — two or three guys I think — "abusing" the driver. One of the guys said to my father, "I hope you have a heart attack and die on the way home." I remember, classic slo-mo, my brother swinging a small bag he was carrying and slamming it into this guy's chest. A scuffle resulted. An actual scuffle. Even in New York it's not often in life that you're close to guys scuffling in actual scuffle, a performance of scuffledom only properly analyzable by scuffology. In an inextricable mixture of cowardice and deep dedication to pacifism, I remember doing nothing for those long seconds until others separated the scufflers, which included my father and my brother. More words exchanged. Threats to call cops. We all went our ways. Sometime later — the ride home? that evening? — some opportune moment later my brother and I went at it about that altercation. He was horrified that I had stood there and done nothing when such words were directed at my father. I was horrified at the use of violence, that he could be goaded into such extreme and destructive behavior by verbal taunt.

There is a link between these anecdotes. In the first two, traveling together, I had goaded my brother into hitting me, taking my money. Here is where he is my cracked mirror, I his. We stood on opposite sides of the looking glass of language and action, neither really understanding each other's position. I had learned how to spiral taunts in concentric circles of painful whorls, creating Vassarellian grids of torment for my brother, who could escape them only by pushing out, lashing out as though those lines were webs he had to break through. Language was tactical, self-defining for me. Though he is an expert punster and highly sensitive to verbal distinctions and colors, it is not primarily my brother's country. On the other hand, I, too often in my life, have not acted, unacted as a person frozen on the Lake of Distinctions and Discriminations, caught in my own world of verbal reaction, disclaiming any act that would change the rage fueling the feelings I could sentence (*sic*) from; I'd mute the anger and keep the surface frozen, turn it up when I couldn't stand the cold impotence of the fact that my words never changed anything. All of which simply adds up to a vicious circle.

My brother acted, and sometimes regretted his actions. I was a watcher, a commentator, who fed on the pain of regret. I use the past tense as though we've resolved all this. Scott and I remain tied together through an umbilical cord of umbrage, shaking between us, as though we came from my father's womb, and only my mother could cut it. Whether or not she would have is moot.

Umbrage, which has always sounded to me like an umbrella-shaped hat, some Magritte creation, takes different forms as one ages. My brother couldn't go on hitting people. He's small and smart. He became a lawyer. I couldn't go on fuming myself into oblivion. I went into therapy; I wrote.

Scott's a successful lawyer: negligence and liability.

I've written these essays: negligence and liability.

There was a time, some narrow window of possibility defined by accident, choice, and other ingredients unknowable and ineffable, when I might have considered law school (argumentation was a Family Value), and Scott might have considered something in the arts, during college, perhaps sophomore year, when the different kinds of knowledge swirling around us seemed to make the idea of one life and one career a cruel joke. We are both might-have-beens — and who knows when the crucial moment flickered, or perhaps the crucial year — and when I see Scott, I often think of how each of us would have managed a version of the other's life. But we both, I think, bowed to the probabilities of our personal evolutionary arcs: like a good conventional biographer, I can say that our careers, read backward, make much sense. Of course biographers can be negligent, but they are rarely liable.

I sometimes want to ask Scott about our time together in memory until I realize that he's been communing with an imaginary David, a version of me, played by Scott in David-clothes, a stirring likeness I will never see. I want to say, on those Ohio–New York telephone calls, "You know the last night we were in our little bedroom, our Balkanized domestic nation; I was ten and you thirteen and I was afraid of going to sleep. Why didn't you comfort me then?" And what could he say but, "Frère, I wasn't there." Nevertheless, all autobiographical essays are epistolary, and I'm trying to say what I haven't said, as well as what I have, imagining along the way what I might: it's an exercise in tense speaking in print to those you love. When I think about my younger self, I almost always find this brother. And I can't help wondering: If those two imagined fellows met, his David and my Scott, would their vulnerability melt them when they kissed? My own memories are such bittersweet *tableau vivants* that I mostly remember them in a kind of appreciative cringe; aren't memories, after all, the lingua Freude of loss?

To wit: this may be the epitome of my childhood relationship with my brother; we followed a counterproductive loop of fighting — something leading to something leading to me crying leading to my father somehow finding out about it. This led to our banishment to our rooms, and worse, a bitter jeremiad about our ingratitude, and a promise that our easy lives of privilege (are children ever responsive to this?) were going to be less privileged, and, one presumes, more difficult.

We're still not sure of whether we fought inordinately, or my father just thought so.

Scott was usually angry at me for letting my father know that we were fighting. This was, of course, always a kind of self-defeating Orwellian coup. As the youngest, I couldn't win a physical fight until my midteens, and couldn't win a verbal fight until . . . I don't know, sometime. But as the oppressed, I needed and felt I needed a way to strike back. I could end the fight on equal terms only by letting my mother or father know. My mother was Yalta, sitting us down to work out a treaty on inevitably inequitable grounds for someone, which was satisfying enough for me, since it still meant cessation. My father was the coup de théâtre, both sides overthrown by a force of nature. This meant that I was desperate for a weapon to fight with, and acted the child's version of Dr. Strangelove, pushing the Leo button, which meant mutually assured destruction. And we rushed for cover: rooms, streets, our mother's skirts, but the fallout always reached us. We would do one of our brotherly Abbott and Costello routines in the logic of childhood:

— If you hadn't told, we wouldn't have been in such trouble.
— If you hadn't hit me, I wouldn't have told.
— I wouldn't have hit you if you had let go of my bike.
— I would have let go of your bike, if you had taken back calling me a fink.
— I wouldn't have called you a fink if you hadn't told.

Beyond a certain age, the circularity of sibling conversations can be breathtakingly silly. I'll let you know when the age has passed. It was puzzling even to us that we could work the postmortem of a fight that had led to such paternal hysteria into another fight that teetered on the edge of a double apocalypse. Perhaps we instinctively realized that my father's anger tended to have one pitch, and it wasn't a slow curve. There wasn't that much else that could be thrown at us. It was at the far edge of one such episode that my brother and I engaged in the sweetest and silliest truce in the history of childhood. As though we were nations on the edge of an epiphany, one summer night — it was light, near-dark — we started discussing one such recent calamity. We must have been in the midst of one of our extended truces, periods of days when we seemed to like each other more than anyone else, where the language of brothers seemed like the only way to talk and really be understood, especially when one had a mercurial father — the patter of pater familias. Sitting on the stoop of our row house, we agreed to never fight again. This was not a detailed treaty, with conditions and contingencies about ending conflict and restoring peace; it was a large-feeling treaty, Gandhian in optimism, rather than an arms pact, with oversight and caution. We shook hands happily and bounced up the stairs to enter the house — Paradise restored? Had it been there to lose? — as two new Adams.

What followed next is for historians to decide. In memories begin responsibilities.

I suppose that means me. I announced to our parents, sitting around the formica dining table, drinking weak tea, that we had reached an agreement to never fight again. I said it triumphantly, with a sense of nobility, as though children like us, or better yet, a child like me, was a thing of such beauty, such temperamental clarity, that parents everywhere should lower their heads as I sauntered by in my Keds. I can almost falsely remember a look of amused pleasure beginning to form on our parents' lips. Turning to face my brother, I saw, prima facie, dismaying evidence of something terribly wrong; his face was twisted sardonically, looking at me as though I were repugnantly stupid. He strode out of the room quickly, muttering under his breath, "You weren't supposed to tell."

I had apparently hit upon the deal breaker: mentioning it. In weeks to come we were to hotly dispute this stipulation, that our treaty was to remain silent (Had my brother been too influenced by the Cuban Missile Crisis? Was I already reacting to Viet Nam?). I felt angry and crestfallen, almost heartbroken that a solution to so many of my problems, a general theory of the family, had so quickly evaporated in a false state of blame.

In the face of what must have felt somewhat miserable, our fighting and my father's myth that our fighting was historically extreme, we attempted a utopian brotherhood. We attempted to literalize Brotherhood. That we shared this desire for love without conflict is the tender heart of this memory. Had we pulled off our plan, we would have been the closest brothers since Romulus and Remus, and would have established, I'm sure, a Brooklyn within Brooklyn, Gravesend as a force to be reckoned with.

Last Exit to Brooklyn

"Last exit to Brooklyn, / Last chance to turn around": the refrain of Gene Pitney's "Last Exit to Brooklyn," one of my favorite New York songs; and the title of Hubert Selby's novel, a most horrifying urban vision. Both refer to the sign leading up to the Verrazano Bridge, my bridge. Urban dwellers have favorite everythings: restaurants, bars, buildings, and yes, even bridges. Most New Yorkers, however, seem to favor the Brooklyn Bridge. It is their favorite bridge in the same way that Christmas is their favorite holiday, an easy call, understandable in its predictability. The Brooklyn Bridge has its dazzling geometry rooted in stone, producing an effect of complicated beauty though a kind of endearingly squat modernism. The Brooklyn Bridge has Hart Crane behind it, over it, in it, poet laureate of the bridge, and *The Bridge*. And its name is full of associations, even for those who can associate next to nothing with it. Don't get me wrong, the Brooklyn is my second favorite bridge in New York, perhaps the world, and let me tell you I've been around. I've seen some bridges in my time. This summer I returned from Rome with six packs of Brooklyn Gum: *gustoluongo*, perhaps ad nauseam. But I need a bridge that hasn't been completely appropriated, that isn't a METAPHOR FOR NEW YORK. This is, of course, part of the problem of writing about New York, and about Brooklyn. It is sometimes posed as a question of saturation (an editor once told me that my subject was too familiar, as though a subject could be, as though I could and should, pragmatically, write autobiographically about a different place, find a bridge to a different past). I'm as offended by the idea that my Brooklyn is others' Brooklyn, as that others' Brooklyn encompasses mine. That said, though, people in self-consciously iconic places look for ways to make it theirs, trading sometimes perversely, sometimes peevishly, in the out of the way, the secondary, the flawed. Or that which has no predating history.

It could be that outright beauty, grace of form, is what I look for in a bridge. This the Verrazano has. Its arc over the Narrows is so soft, so subtle, that it seems to echo the curve of sky, with a suppleness even in its name. Of course it is has a z in the middle, as do I, making it my slant-rhyming namesake.

I don't resent the Verrazano for replacing the ferry, and I loved the ferry. But I grew up with the Verrazano, by it, and this has much to do with my affections. The Brooklyn Bridge was loved for generations before I was slapped into Bensonhurst and bridge awareness. But I can legitimately claim, that is, indisputably claim, to have been the first person to love the Verrazano Bridge. I remember its supports, jutting hunks of potential, waiting to cover the Belt Parkway. I remember my young wonder at the structure in progress, and loving both my wonder and the sense of process. Each time we would drive the Belt to Manhattan, a little more of the bridge was finished. But for a long time it seemed that construction was ongoing only on the Brooklyn side — the Staten Island side was too distant to see, or to take particular note of. It seemed generous that Brooklyn was extending out, giving a way for others to come to it. Since I think I only thought of the bridge, in its early stages, as a way in to Brooklyn. After all, who would willingly choose to go to Staten Island? I thought of Staten Island as the Devil's Island of New York. People were sent there, probably for ghastly civic crimes: taking the name of New York in vain, or spitting, or soliciting, whatever that was.

Though I was the first person to love the bridge, I was not the first to love under it. My time came later, twelve years later, in 1974, my senior year in high school, with the only other person I had ever met who knew who Cisco Houston, Phil Ochs, Leadbelly, Woody Guthrie were. We discovered this unlikely association of interests on the D Train to Manhattan, my seventeenth birthday and our first date: Bob Dylan at Madison Square Garden, echoes of *Lay Lady Lay* jostling for attention in my inner ear with *Love Minus Zero/No Limits*. As portentous as this was, or seemed at the time, the route to our romantic initiation was utterly baroque.

When I was a precocious fourteen, I was co-leader of canvassing for the McGovern campaign in my Brooklyn district. For the first half of the summer, I worked side by side with a girl two years my senior, Sonnet Takahisa (was there ever a more alluring name?), on the boardwalk in Manhattan Beach, Brighton Beach, up to Coney Island, giving out literature and talking up McGovern (a politician I remember loving, just as I did my other early enthusiasms: Ramsey Clark, Bella Abzug, stretching back to Bobby Kennedy, my premier amour politique). One morning in 1968, my mother, brother, and I sat watching a Kennedy news conference on TV. My brother and I were begging my mother to promise to vote for him. She said it depended on his answer to a question about Israel.

When the answer proved satisfactory, my brother and I shouted, "Hurray, hurray, Mom's going to vote for Bobby!" Six months later we visited California, and stayed at the Ambassador, weeks after Bobby had been shot there, devastating me, and making me deeply hate the entire nation as much as any politically aware eleven-year-old could. We were walking down the street, and I ran ahead to pick up a newspaper for my father, since newspapers were our family Bible — we got them all, and cited them throughout the day. The headline read: Russian tanks invade Czechoslovakia. I knew, with a sad tenderness that rendered me hypersensitive to the plight of all oppressed people, beginning with myself, that Prague Spring was over that summer.

Sonnet Takahisa — the digression allows me to repeat the name. Our boardwalk audience was almost completely composed of concentration camp survivors. We were earnest and passionate, and not at all uncomfortable by the rows upon rows of elderly survivors, arms browning in the sun to a more muted frame for their blue camp tattoos. We explained that we were against the war. We explained that we were against the bomb. We made clear that we need a good, decent, sane man in the White House who cared about people. Our listeners were mostly bemused, especially by me, a chubby fourteen-year-old zealot, trying to throw a word or two of Yiddish out to make my message personal: Nixon's *tsoris*, he's a *meshuganah*. McGovern's a *mensch*. I remember thinking these people must care; and I remember thinking that I might be bothering them, annoying their time in the sun, the simple, hot sun. They were mostly polite, occasionally waved me away.

That summer, my family and I were in Hong Kong, Leo and Waterman having gotten us bargain-basement fares, hotels, drivers, and cars in Japan and Thailand, as well. The four of us were walking down a street in Kowloon, and who should be strolling toward us? Sonnet Takahisa, with her little sister and parents. Sonnet, who lived four

Brooklyn blocks away from me, and from whom I had separated after our political pas de deux without exchanging information on what we were doing the rest of the summer. I had been utterly smitten with her; she was my beautiful half-Jewish, half-Japanese pagan goddess with a social conscience. But she was two years older, thin, and did I mention beautiful? An intoxicating canvassing partner, but clearly out of my league. And here she was, like a strange Coney Island distorting mirror set down in the Far East, mirroring my family with the perfect symmetry of two girl children walking toward two boy children; this was Kismet if there ever was. But my mark was off just a bit. Though we exchanged phone numbers, and our parents friendly amused greetings, I never saw her again. She was days away from starting college, Radcliffe, no less, and when I turned the lights down low and called her, had no time to meet me. Three years later, though, in high school, her little sister Wendy appeared before me again, a transmogrified vision — a gift to my older, slimmer self. We smirked and shook hands, joked that *"It was so lovely to see you in Hong Kong, and how have you been?"*

Then Dylan, and a month later we found the bridge together, and it was our bridge for a number of months. The bridge, in that time, crystallized as a female form, whereas before it had been so only vaguely. It became my intercessor and her chaperone: I thought its religious grace smoothed the transition underneath peasant blouses and peasant skirts; she believed no sacrilege possible under the shadow of its protective presence. Framed by the windshield of the dark car, it was an icon of beautiful permission, permissible beauty, Our Lady of the Lustful Narrows. I remember rainy nights, the summer of '74, rows of cars off the Belt and by the bridge, little mobile pleasure domes, each with young and not-so-young couples, utterly private in public, and I remember feeling the Narrows water without hearing it, smelling it, hearing the occasional gull cry, and knowing the bridge was looming like an enigmatic promise. Being in a car by your favorite bridge, on a night when first love is that sweet ache and the pressure in your loins is an innocent need for *everything,* when your Wendy opens up partly to her Peter Pan, when you kiss a love's bead of sweat for the first time . . . is a bridge to memory that you couldn't lose if you tried. And why, in Verrazano's name, would you ever try?

The Verrazano did not bear witness to the painful conclusion of my first great love, several months later. What happened? Everyone's favorite and most painful question. It's a question that haunts one of my favorite movie memories — the end of *The Sand Pebbles*, with Steve McQueen. He's shot the snipers aiming at him on the roof of a missionary compound, and wants nothing more than to leave, to rejoin his ship and Candace Bergen (a combination only slightly less alluring than the Verrazano and Wendy Takahisa). McQueen's eyes, always underrated in their complex register, seemed to have noted the numbers, and he's got a single, long hall to run down to an open door, and he's tense but thinks he's clear. His eyes say all this. He takes two steps, maybe three, a shot rings out and he falls. He leans against something, I forget exactly what, and his eyes are now glassy, but angry and unbelieving. "I was clear," he says. "What happened? What the hell happened?" One more shot hits him, and he's through. This scene has spooked me for almost thirty years, because what the hell happened is the toughest question, and even its answers are frequently no consolation. I know that Wendy's mother was appalled at how "serious" we were. My mother, I believe, was in utter distress, in jealous distress of displacement, that I cared about another female. We never would have admitted this, but at seventeen and fifteen we had already mapped out our lives together, and figured out the earliest we could possibly get married. I told no one this either, but skipped going out of state to college my freshman year, attending NYU so I wouldn't have to leave my sweetheart. Her parents took her to South America for a month to put some distance between us. Before she left, she left me a letter for each day she would be gone, thirty letters, lightly scented, housed in a green box. Every evening, around dusk, I would pull my letter for the day and drive out the Belt to the bridge, to Verrazano. The lovers in adjacent cars were lingering, impatiently loitering, waiting for the cover of darkness. But you could see them brushing arms, exchanging light kisses full of deeper expectation. I'd open my letter for my daily fix of "I love you I love you I love you and nothing will ever keep us apart and I miss you and our bridge." The bridge, my personal saint and bridely canopy, had become ours, and I felt a pang about this, as though something had been taken away, replaced of course by desperate necessity, but losses to great feelings are less losses for that.

There I was, the bridge, the sky, and me all growing dusky, but only I was longing with a sharp pain. When Wendy returned, we both felt strange, though she was more game to ride it out. I had a most strange and estranging experience, also by water, several weeks later. We took the Day Line up to Bear Mountain, the scene of one of our most intense times together, months earlier. This was an attempt to recreate the magic, something I've since learned should be attempted only with the greatest care, since failure is full of deadly possibilities. We were walking along a stream I loved to picnic by, and I was overwhelmed by a sensation of vertigo mixed with sorrow. I told my sweet I had to lean against a rock for a minute, and she anxiously begged me to tell her what was wrong. I couldn't speak for several minutes, but looking back I can only describe what I felt as a kind of negative epiphany, a dark version of a Wordsworthian spot of time. I felt a spiraling sense of the absence of feeling, a sharp and lonesome negation. Ironically, I felt, more keenly than I ever have in my life (though I was to experience versions of this again), that I could feel nothing. When the dizziness had passed, I felt somehow that I was no longer in love. I know it sounds strange, almost pathological and almost occult, as though we had walked past a malevolent wood sprite, some postmodern Mordred who lived to kill the best illusions, but that's just what I experienced. It's easily enough pyschologized: the desperate first passion, the pressure of parents, the separation, my sense of anxiety about having chosen not to go away to college, which I had been planning for years, the almost impossible repetition of a scene of romantic intensity . . . but I didn't know what hit me then, and I remain unwilling to box my understanding of myself in too neatly. This sounds resistant, I believe, but I also believe in not forcing conclusions on my younger selves, who are, after all, unable to compete fairly in the enterprise. So, what the hell happened? How did I go from bridge love to stream loss? It's a shot in the dark, as Steve McQueen might say with his eyes. Not that there aren't answers, but that the single-gunman theory of love's assassination is never completely convincing. I'm left here on a hot afternoon in the summer of '99, landlocked in the Midwest far from bridges and Brooklyn, trying to decipher the importance of the grassy knoll where reasons for what I felt as a boy might linger, without splendor, in the grass.

Wendy and I lingered for a few weeks more, and I finally said I needed to not see her anymore. The whole time I kept feeling "I don't feel the same," and less than what I felt is horrible to feel. Though I might have found in the Verrazano a maternal poise to soothe, I avoided the bridge for months, avoided creating an association I thought would be hard to shake, which, I feared, could drive a wedge between us, the bridge and me. It became mine again, when a suitable interval passed, but it did not claim me, I merely returned to it. Neither diffident nor threatening, the bridge made no demands, asked only that I come to her, notice the span, and consider how long we had known each other.

Leaving Verrazano was the hardest part of my drive to California, over twenty years ago. My tiny Fiat and I were embarking west, where I would begin graduate school at Stanford in 1978. It was a humid and rainy Tuesday afternoon. I was determined to begin the drive despite an ankle severely sprained by "one last game" of basketball on the broken-up courts near Brighton Beach. A nod to the past before the open promise of a new state. My first stop would be D.C., to spend a few desultory days with the woman I had been seeing, who was in the middle of law school and almost-loved me while I kind of liked her. To get to her I had to pass through the arms of Verrazano, and confront her sign. Bits of the song's lyrics scattered through my mind like the fickle swings of a flag in bridge wind: "I'm leaving now for parts unknown. . . . these wheels of mine are turning, churning. . . . She hurt me for the very last time. . . ." Naturally, the refrain weaved in and out, the pattern of cars switching lanes on a highway, a bridge as seen from the air: "Last exit to Brooklyn, / Last chance to turn around."

I thought I heard something snap when the car emerged from the Verazzano to the now-neutral turf of Staten Island, gateway to New Jersey, and the West.

I thought of Verrazano in Jersey and Pennsylvania, with my girl-friend in Washington ("Is there someone else?"), Virginia, Missouri, Kansas, Colorado. . . . I thought of her in every state. It was only in the Sierras, at the California checkpoint, that I felt the bridge and I were truly reconciled. The border guard (really a fruit and wildlife inspector) asked me where I was coming from, what my destination was. This increased my sense of moving to another country, being in a different land. I told her I was coming from the Verrazano Bridge. She shrugged, nodded. I think she understood, though she neither laughed, nor smiled. When I crossed the Golden Gate, my heart started racing and my car felt like it was going much too fast. It was the most beautiful view from a bridge I had ever seen, the Bay seeming to cradle the city. But it was still not the most beautiful bridge itself, and I sensed Verrazano forgave me at that moment, for not turning around.

Season of Love . . . .

n my excursions into memory, those times when I will myself into the past, frequently I find myself at the door of the incipient. Those just-about-to-happen memories, whether they happened or not, pull me to an excruciating point of truth, demand that I try to arrange and rearrange details into a form that satisfies, that seems to satisfy the need to see just what happened. Then comes the easy part: figuring out what it means.

I was twenty, just out of college, talking to a friend on the telephone. Having gotten off early from work, a research job for a Manhattan foundation, I was enjoying the pleasing banter that comes from talking to someone at exactly the right intervals. This friend and I, some years earlier, had silently reached the understanding that we could not bond bosom to bosom as we had in early adolescence, but needed to stay within each other's orbits. It was a warm afternoon; I paced the cool dark carpet of the first floor of my parents' row house, saying and listening to familiar phrases, familiar names. I had an appointment to meet another friend, Richie Ernst, at Manhattan Beach for some basketball, but that was an hour away. I had time for pleasantries, for oldfriendtalk.

The door to the staircase always needed planing. It was at the top of the stairs. The stairs themselves numbered twelve carpeted steps down and two to the right. This put you in the "playroom," a misnomer since we never used it for anything but storage. The first floor of the house had been my grandparents' apartment. When they died, the staircase became the connection to a sane level of space. My brother and I were liberated from one cramped room to two smallish rooms whose comparative space impressed us through our adolescences to the time we left home. The only vestige of the grandparent days down in our new country was an enormous mirror that seemed to occupy half of one wall of the playroom. My mother yelled down, "Richie's here."

"Send him down," I said, thinking it odd that my friend should be here when I was to meet him there.

The door to the staircase thudded open. Steps down the stairs. I continued talking but moved to where I could see my friend emerge. But he didn't. Standing on the small landing was a young man, middle twenties, long blond hair in tresses, and piled high. His loose shirt was open, his chest hairless. We stood looking at each other for ten or twenty seconds. I did not know him. I said, "Hold on," said it to the phone and set it down. I experienced a pure cognitive dissonance, unlike any confusion I had known. My mind started racing: friend of my brother, someone whom I didn't recognize . . . nothing fit. Finally: "Do I know you?" He stepped down the two steps and walked toward me; he was a foot away. He extended his hand. Dazed, I shook it, and as I did he announced, calmly, pleased, "This is the season of love."

"Who are you?"

"This is the season of love."

"Do I know you?"

"This is the season of love."

"What do you want?"

"This is the season of love."

He wanted me to turn around and look into my grandparents' mirror. "Just look in the mirror," he kept repeating, as though that would explain everything, as though I would see something, some sign, some manifestation of the season of love. Then there was silence, house silence, the non-noise of the inside of something. I trembled, and a sense of cognizance started returning. Even so, I contemplated looking into the mirror. It was a tantalizing charge, an almost attractive imperative. Not only that, but I have never excelled in physical confrontations, unless they called for passivity, pliancy. If the rule, clear, were that I was to give in, play dead, as a means of extrication, I could do that, did do that well. No one could have been robbed, hassled, bullied as much as I was, and escaped so relatively unscathed, without some acumen, some Eastern impulse that shut the systems down, yielded what was wanted, and went on its shaken but unbroken way. I had internalized a confrontational decorum, and felt it welling up, urging me to turn and gaze at the glass.

But I could not turn, or I would not: in my memory a combination of pride and paralysis, indistinguishable.

My next reaction: I started yelling, repeating over and over, "Get out get out get out get out get out get out." I edged him to the door, I'm not sure how, and in one swift movement pushed him out, my territory restored, the witch in the oven. I went upstairs to interrogate my mother.

"Where's your friend?"

"He's gone. Why did you let him in?"

"He came to the door and said, 'I'm a friend of your son.' I said, 'You mean David?' He said, 'Yes, David.' He said his name was Richie."

"You nearly got me killed. He was no one I knew."

This became a family joke. The intruder was for a while variously referred to as my boyfriend — Richie Rich, my brother called him — Charles Manson, others I have forgotten. The story-ness had limited appeal, apparently. It faded from the canon of family tales, no doubt in part because I rejected the happy ending. And I rejected the happy ending because I had to live with the mirror, which became all mirrors. I had mirror dreams for some months, sometimes playing Alice, pushed through the glass to a side identical to the real side. Unreversed, it felt like an unbearable distortion. In one dream, only my head went through, my shoulders absorbing the shards of the fickle mirror. Sometimes I would turn to the mirror but lose the dream before I could behold what was in it. What a perfectly existential motif, to have had to deal with the mirror so, as though this was exactly the torment that was wished, as though my visitor was a dybbuk who had read Sartre and Lewis Carroll. Six months later, though, I was living in California, the mirror covered in my mind by a myriad of distractions. As luck would have it, I found a small studio apartment with a single bathroom cabinet mirror. My hair lightened, I grew thin with exercise and tasteless organic cuisines, and I loosened my tightly buttoned shirts.

Rear Windows

imagined Raymond Burr stalking my stairway, a quick cut to the doorknob turning. Lights out; I reach for my flash camera in a clever but only temporary gambit to save my life. Grace Kelly pulls Raymond Burr off me, and I am instantly relieved of both voyeurism and psychic impotence. At least this is, in somewhat compressed and distorted sequence, how I remembered Hitchcock's *Rear Window*. I somehow doubt that James Stewart's injury was a ruptured tendon from a game of basketball, long delayed by the natural sloth of aging nonathletes, nor does it seem likely that his injury was laden with the overly ironic detail of having occurred at a new Houston facility for the handicapped. I did, however, live on the second floor, in an apartment almost crazy with windows, and had a beautiful girlfriend who may or may not be destined to marry into European royalty. I also had some suspicious, possibly demented neighbors, and so, ponderously, I connected my helplessness and frustration with Hitchcock's implicit thesis on psychosexual debilitation, simply a situational connection, of course.

I have always acted like a wounded animal when sick or hurt. Spurning sympathy and convalescent care, I prefer to crawl into a little room, or perhaps commute between a few of them, slowly, quietly, and mend and emerge whole. It feels like stopping time, entering a world where increments of physical recuperation are the only believable measurements. Three days, five days, the body ages ever so slightly as it becomes sanguine, in a confusion, a contradiction of aging. When the recovery is extended, the necessary narcissism accompanying healing intensifies and may become self-conscious; we watch ourselves licking our wounds.

I have ruptured my Achilles tendon. I enjoyed saying that. A rupture is so dramatic that it sounds irremediable, and more miraculous somehow that one can be put, or sewn, back together. Such good company to be in for an injury, too. Other than this *aristeia* of arrested movement, what will I or any other mortal or half-mortal ever share with the sacker of Troy? *Sing, Goddess.* And put a word in to Hypocrites for me. Tell this medicinal god that I'm flattered, and ready to move on.

Other than trips to my supposedly crackerjack, though frighteningly nonverbal Med Center surgeon, I did not leave my apartment for the first two weeks after my injury. Fortunately, my section of Houston, Montrose, could always promise some action on the street, some little psychodrama boiling over, to bring the outside in from time to time. O Montrose in July, through thirteen windows. Unlucky for all but a voyeur, even if stirred circumstantially. My voyeurism was mostly aural. "Coco, Coco," the woman down the block must be mad. Is that really a dog she calls? Is she, in fact, a woman? Have I grown so used to transvestism that such conundrums of neighborly metamorphosis no longer fascinate? It is the voice of the world, merely, I decided. The shuffling feet on the stairs at four A.M., while I was watching *Sleeper* on TV, another insomniacal night, intrigued me for only two or three nights. They were objects of envy though, those feet. I wish I could shuffle, I thought. If I could shuffle, I could slide; if I could slide, I could skate; if I could skate, I could . . . tango? And then I could surely walk, and cure myself of apartment fever.

I grew tired, very tired, of air-conditioning. Houston summers — that killing floor of heat that at its worst seems piped down from some upper-atmospheric rending plant — sometimes seem a necessary invention offering relief from the dead frigid air pumped into apartments and doctors' offices. "O rend the heat," the poet H.D. writes, and it sometimes seems that some demented entrepreneur has taken her seriously. But I was almost beyond exigencies of climate control, of any control other than the emotional temper of waiting, and this, too, strained as I began to leave on little-attended jaunts. I could not drive, for months, and so I accumulated a small cadre of chaperones, driving duennas who would lend me an arm, accompany me from house to house, or market, or the bank. The natural world became movielike: fast-forward through car windows, or the freeze-frames of my apartment. But among the things that got old was the asking for help, so I spent days inside and alone, becoming too intimate with my apartment, risking residential estrangement.

There was plenty of time to replay my injury, and to see where it belonged in my canon of stupidity and carelessness. I indulged in days spent watching those inner movies, doing nothing else. I remembered an incident I believe I sculpted at the time to stir future rue. When I was sixteen, I decided to dare the elements. It was a languorous summer of only occasional employment. The worst summer day in New York history hit. It was one hundred and six degrees. The foul air hung heavily, slowly sapping the world of energy. Everything must simply combust if the heat held for one more moment, or fold up into an unspeakable miasma. But instead of yielding gracefully to the hot earth, paying it homage, I decided to take my body to the playground and play basketball, simply because I could. Having shed the weight of several skins a bare two years earlier, I was still in the throes of wonderment at my new body. I decided that this slimmer and still-young version of myself could survive the heat, but might never be able to again so challenge fate and the elements, assert the body's vitality with such arrogance. Averse as I was then and always to high places, roller coasters, not to mention the very idea of jumping out or climbing up, it was my customized and controlled form of thrill seeking: assured, and probably for one time only. At the park I met my double, Lester Block, whom I hadn't seen for years, and who had also lost much weight, though not with such transfiguring drama, had had the same idea. Together we formed a small and loose community of the metabolically bold. We paid for our perverse assertions with labored moves, weak shots that seemed to sink as soon as they left the hand. But we played it out, and then played it up, a freakish display of bravado. I said to myself, This You Will Remember. In the Hall of Fame of memories you have added a trophy.

The trophy turned into a gauntlet that has hit me at ten-year intervals, more or less. On my first visit to Houston, almost twenty years ago, I went gamely with some friends to play basketball on an unshaded court in West University. It was noon and it was August, and I lasted five minutes before, retching and near-numb, I crawled from the court to the shade in a dangerous imitation of heatstroke.

It was with a sense of irony, and nothing at stake, that a friend and I tried the new Center on West Gray during the worst part of our recent tropical depression. Wearing a sense of silliness on our short sleeves, we tested ourselves slowly, while the storm was at its peak. I have so blithely mistreated my body for years that nothing seemed at stake; there was nothing I could prove, I reasoned. We were inside and careful, dry and slow and safe.

Two days after this trial run came the fateful play, with two more players, soon to become witnesses. I was much too tired to keep on, but what could happen if I did? In the third game of round-robin, my tall teammate set a long pick, just outside the three-point line. I jumped, and the inner acoustics of my body echoed a succinct and telling pop; I seemed to float down with a spot just about my heel completely soft and shocked and swelling. When I hit the floor I turned to see who had thrown the brick at the back of my heel. Then I clawed at my sneaker, furiously trying to take it off. I felt both intense pain and estrangement from my foot. Another species would have used its teeth.

A week later, after surgery, my friend of the Sturm-and-Drang game came over to memorialize my condition. He warned me not to use my crutches as a crutch. That heat-bearing light of late afternoon was strong enough, even with thirteen drawn blinds, for photographs. He did not need a flash, but took several shots for insurance. Later that night, my girlfriend and I debated a trip out to rent *Rear Window*. She kept looking at me, and I kept looking at my leg. Then it was too late. When I dragged myself to bed, after she had gone, I felt old and heavy and unclear. I dropped into sleep like quicksilver, though, and dreamed I was a young man in heat.

My Little Heroes

ne of my first memories of the movies is somewhat in-
cestuous. I remember walking into my parents' bedroom
in our row house in Brooklyn, the black-and-white TV
screen throwing light from a corner. My parents were
supine, each on his and her sides of their trundle bed. They
were murmuring, talking in that affectless tone of remark-
ing that people use when the tube is on and they're actually watching it. Their heads were toward the door, and they couldn't
see me come in. I wanted to get closer, to hear what connubial words
were being exchanged in the bluish TV-screen light. A movie was
showing, something from the forties or thirties, a mansion, men in
evening dress, women in dressy dresses. I moved closer and heard my
father's voice more clearly; he was saying things like Joseph Schild-
kraut, S. Z. Sakall, Marjorie Main, James Gleason, Patsy Kelly, Elisha
Cook, Edward Everett Horton. He was naming the characters who
swirled around the margins, never far from the lead actors, but were
sometimes on and off after one brief line, one double take, a short verbal effusion or a bit of physical business.

I looked at my parents, looked at the screen, back and forth. How
could they know the names of such unimportant players? Why would
they? Sometimes little grunts and groans of delight seemed to urge out
of them at the mention of a particular name. I tiptoed out, and wondered how these people had spent their lives, and why they didn't have
a door that locked.

Little did I know that I would find myself, decades later, engaged in
a similar pursuit, although the room is larger, the TV in color, the mattress singularly firm and large, no one stepping up stealthily while I
watch, and miles from Brooklyn before I sleep.

Ward Bond, Beulah Bondi, Arthur Treacher. Character actors all. And a related category: the second leads, who may or may not be character actors. I've always loved those second leads who stuck around long enough to take the lead, even if, or perhaps especially when, these vocational promotions were never quite convincing: Joel McCrae, Don Ameche, Eddie Bracken. Of course, there is the occasional actor or actress who blurs the line: Van Johnson (and I may be the only remaining Van Johnson fan under a certain age, his portrait of grief in *The Last Time I Saw Paris* almost unwatchably good, his line readings spoken with a kind of tartness that would get Tom Cruise slapped), or Gloria Grahame, who won an Oscar, had a long career with name sometimes above the title, but never transcended a certain sultriness, which is why she is in my pantheon of Hollywood sirens. The character actor who becomes and stays a star is epitomized by Judy Holliday, with whom I would gladly run off to Tahiti or the Bronx, were she not, unfortunately, dead. She is the only actress I know who can completely pull off a goofy sexuality without undermining either quality.

Since I can't run away with Judy Holliday, I may as well fully endorse a fictive turn of mind and marry off my two all-time favorite character actors, my cinematic parents: Edward Everett Horton and Jessie Royce Landis. But before we reach the nuptials, lest anyone object, perhaps I should explain why these two are, in my book, heroic, and why they are going to have a strange and delightful lifetime together in my mind. They are heroic because I do not have much of an appreciation of conventional heroism. Hold that: I should say, instead, that it doesn't interest me terribly. Instead of the idea of noble and inspiring acts, I am much more drawn to interesting and endearing people. Others laud character, but I tend to laud characters who are heroic to me in the way they expand the human franchise of individuality, even peculiarity, or embody qualities I find underrepresented, or unique in combination. That is my idea, and as Eric Idle of Monty Python says, when asked what it is: it is mine.

My parents will be united by a unique blend of sophisticated xenophobia. They are savvy Americans in their way, these two, the bewildered nouveau riche, and have an aversion to foreign culture, especially French, which they submit to out of a comical sense that it is where one goes if one has to — to do business, for example: managing the great Petrov (Fred Astaire) in *Shall We Dance?* in Horton's case; or to show one's "finished" daughter the world, as is the case with Landis in *To Catch a Thief.* In the former case, in Paris, Horton asks, "Où est Petrov?" with the consternation of a man for whom language is a minefield that one must walk across and a foreign language a minefield that one must crawl across. In the latter, Landis, at a surreally elaborate costume party on the Riviera, drops her sense of masquerade to ask a bartender, memorably, "Avez-vous bourbon?" — the third word inflected with the pique of a woman who is so comfortable being herself that any pretense is a chore requiring a foolproof and homegrown tonic. They move in heady circles, these two, and their clothes are tailored and expensive, but they are resolutely unpretentious. And that is the central reason my parents don't like France.

My own father was rather ego-strong, overbearing, and I sometimes think it would be lovely to have a witty, slightly befuddled, somewhat impotent father who could also do world-class double takes. He would, of course, be impotent in the right way: a detestosteroned personality or, in conventional terms, gentle, neither overengaged nor underinvolved, with three-piece tweed suits that looked pretty natty on his pear-shaped body.

Their voices: his has a squeak that comes and goes, a bit of patrician New York, with a steady waver, and an unexpectedly musical effect, up and down the scales; her voice is mezzo, the accent hints at a lower class that has moved up, rounded out, a Boston Brahmin via Dubuque, and when she speaks you feel her sense of balanced certainty, and that this certainty is as qualified as anything else, which is to say *rather.*

He proves it is possible to be heroically flustered. She shows a heroically mature feminine sexuality.

His tie is askew, and his shoes come untied. Her dress is satin, a strap hangs off one fifty-five-year-old shoulder.

Her eyes widen suggestively. His narrow perplexedly.

My heroic father does not wander like Odysseus, but he is very amusing while looking for his socks. My heroic mother does not sacrifice interminably, and she looks smashing in a long silk robe, with matching slippers that she mocks.

He's slightly bent, but, surprisingly, wears clothes well, a tux that he claims is uncomfortable, or three-piece tweed that really is jaunty. His fedora's at an angle, and damn if he doesn't look almost handsome, despite a nose that vies with his brim for prominence. And he moves with fluidity, which his awkward body would never suggest.

In *To Catch a Thief*, the Cat, Cary Grant, is under quiet threat of seduction by Grace Kelly, an absurd idea, but perhaps the only possible response to such cool perfection is resistance — that or prostration. The famous kiss outside her hotel room, the two having just met: she takes him head in hands and plants one on him, and he looks like the cat who swallowed a canary. It's the same look of sexual luck that Grant also flashes on the train to Eva Marie Saint in *North by Northwest*, when she says that she never makes love before eating. But it is the mother's, Jessie Royce Landis's, seduction of the Cat for her daughter that I'm . . . more seduced by, her casual air of what's wrong with you for not making love to my beautiful daughter? And while seducing the Cat as a suitor for her daughter, with the indefatigable air of someone who recognizes that the sexual arts have entered a decadent and altogether clumsy age, Landis flirts beautifully with Cary Grant herself, culminating in the moment that will always, for me, be "the look": the Cat is searching her hotel room for signs of the copy Cat he is tracking. He turns to Jessie Royce Landis and says, "You must sleep soundly." She says, "I do," a matrimonial avowal, but with the flicker of a smirk and the slow closing of eyes saying even more. Quite frankly, what they say is the word *fuck* in every possible permutation. It isn't quite an invitation, although it verges. And it is much deeper than a boast. It's an unflinching assertion of sexual prowess, made to a potential son-in-law, who it just so happens, is almost exactly her age, in fact is a few months older. As Cary Grant's mother in *North by Northwest*, Landis is therefore younger than her son. This is delightful, but improbable, practically impossible. If Landis is a heroine of sexual self-knowledge and droll self-mockery, considering the situation, she would almost have to be.

To interrupt a laugh with a jolt of self-knowledge usually means you've learned the joke's on you. One turns *Isn't that amusing* into *Aren't I a fool*. But to do with a sense of comic dignity, to signal indignity with dignity, is the quality that holy fools possess. They can change laughs in midstream. Horton's version of this, though, isn't sentimental; it's the urban version, and it's ultimate message is that sophistication is a quality of limited value. "Elia, thou art sophisticated," Charles Lamb says to himself in a bemused moment of recognition. In Edward Everett Horton's case, we think, in gratitude, *Thou can never be sophisticated*.

His head strides into a room ahead of his body, the cane he carries looking more like a tail than an accoutrement. She moves languorously and knowingly in clothes that few can afford and few care less about. For Horton, the art of indignation usually involves a midair correction. He agrees, wholeheartedly, until he realizes that he disagrees completely. In *Shall We Dance?*, a classic example of how the simplest series of utterances can be riotously original, especially when spoken with a sincerity that belies any attempt to be casually pusillanimous, Horton says, in response to a question meant to elicit his guilt: "Yes. That is, not exactly. No." The line sums up the film's ambivalent attempt to unite high and low culture, ballet and tap dancing, by clicking sharply with comic elegance. Even though Horton wants his friend and client, the great Petrov, to continue with the art of the ballet, he makes us understand that no one who acts as adamantly confused as he could represent a pure and stultifying ideology. His confusion liberates Fred Astaire, frees up free love and the love of mixed artistic forms, and sets in motion my hyperextended analysis of this piece of popular culture.

The scene of laughter and forgetting, in the elevator, in *North by Northwest*: Cary Grant cannot convince his mother — Jesse Royce Landis — doing a more tart reprise of her role in *To Catch a Thief* — that he is in danger. Crowded into a hotel elevator with the men who want to kill him. Landis looks at the men and asks if they are trying to kill her son. Her delivery of the line is the machina of the scene: very American in its directness, but with more than a hint of absurdity. She starts laughing, as does every other woman on the elevator. The laughter goes from a slightly giddy disbelief to a kind of hysteria, the killers heartily joining in. Everyone is laughing but her son, Cary Grant (who, remember, is older than his mother). This is the stuff of nightmares, specifically Freudian ones. Okay, it's certainly one of mine. But how else, after all, could one respond to a son's public avowal that two men huddled close in a small room moving downward are cold killers? It sounds like a joke, so it must be one. Landis-Mother's infectious laughter is castrating, but ultimately creates the dramaturgical extravagance of Grant's exit, his escape. Her laughter is the indulgence of unalloyed skepticism, and is extended by the hilarity in her eyes, their combination of innocence and experience — a particularly American marriage of naivete and knowingness. Lest a mother's disbelief in her son's turmoil, his potentially fatal mistaken identity, be perceived as unheroic, it is important to note that her skepticism is a function of his own character flaw, his failure to invest authentically in anything. And despite her witheringly witty responses to the quagmire of confusion and danger he has gotten himself into, she can be cajoled into helping him, all along acting as though life were quite strange in a most normal way, and these particulars were merely an extension of life's normally wacky vicissitudes. Landis is, in other words, a heroine of the oedipally surreal. The perfect Hitchcock mother.

And surreal will describe her wedding to Edward Everett Horton (the ceremony performed, perhaps, by Jacques Tati? He's French, true, but never speaks). I can hardly wait to see Landis's face, or perhaps to hear her laugh. Horton will murmur, "Oh, dear," and she will look at him with muted astonishment, not quite sure of how she got there, not quite sure of why I'm doing this to her, but with a sense of the weirdness of fate. She'll acknowledge she did *something* to put her in this predicament, or she might just find the whole thing terribly amusing. Horton will announce himself as ready as he'll ever be. I know that he can handle a strong woman, since his marriage with Susan (played by Ruth Donnelly) in *Holiday* is one of the great screen relationships. I do feel a bit like a cinematic home-wrecker. This couple has inspired me for decades, much as it inspires Cary Grant and Katharine Hepburn in the 1938 film (the film was first made in 1930, with Horton playing the same role). What makes this marriage magical is what also makes Grant and Hepburn so good together: a sense of play suggesting a profound knowledge of one's partner. It sounds simple until you realize that cosmic chemistry sets are almost never on sale. This is Horton's best role, his meatiest, because he gets to play to his intelligence as a professor, as unlikely as that combination may sometimes seem, as opposed to his delightful but slighter roles in many other films. Wit and affection are the household gods here, and Horton invokes them with the élan of a seasoned practitioner. Horton and Donnelly, and Grant and Hepburn — thanks to James Barrie's play, Donald Ogden Stewart's script, George Cukor's usual finesse with actors — make a usually graceful though sometimes heavy-handed attack on class pretensions, and no scene displays this more amusingly than Horton's losing his shoe in a galosh to an overattentive butler, and trying obsequiously, and then determinedly, to retrieve it as he limps around a grand foyer that impresses him as impressively unfamiliar. "It seems to have been a residence of some kind at one point," he says drolly to his wife.

It is in *Holiday* that Horton is most heroic, in my terms, and his performance here, which was I'm sure the first of his I ever saw, has colored every subsequent performance I've seen. It is heroic because it is honorable and eccentric. He is amusingly, dedicatedly himself, devoted to those he loves, and free of institutional investment. Note some wishful thinking on my part? What are heroes for? After all, I find the idea of running into burning buildings a miracle of adrenalized fear-repression, and have been unimpressed with most "great deeds" since I was eleven, finding in most a self-aggrandizing quality that makes me queasy.

No, Horton and Landis will be quite happy together. I believe they'll have an active sex life, fueled by good humor, and they won't take any guff from anyone who pretends to more than their own very American, slightly kooky, occasionally sharp-tongued vision of character. I'm proud of my parents, and if they ain't heroic, pour me an epic and pass the ammunition, but keep the lights down low so we can still see the screen: my father in black and white, my mother in color.

Family Snaps

*Not having been a drug addict, an alcoholic or a psycho, I don't need
a ghost writer. . . . I began as a dark-room man.*

— Weegee (Arthur Fellig), An Autobiography

first began thinking of family photographs as a genre when I
noticed how intolerant I had become of their literary use. More
specifically, it seems that twenty-five years ago, more or less,
American poets started writing family photograph poems with
an alarming frequency. There were a few motifs that recurred
constantly: grandmothers on porches, mothers by windows,
first communions. What bothered me about these poems was
the tone of reverent lyricism, nostalgia for an age of filtered sunlight
on hazy days, and the predictability with which the photographs
seemed to illuminate complete lives, almost as if the photograph were
not merely tremendously portentous, but somehow responsible as
well. The impulse was generous: to preserve and commemorate. In
doing so, one could find the key to relationships, understand and reveal oneself. But photographs are problematic evidence, cropped experience. Of course, so is memory, but its subjectivity is more obvious.
Or it should be.

The impulse to poeticize when looking at family snapshots is
strong, and strong, too, the resistance to ironize the past when it seems
palpable; nostalgia shoots into memory's bloodstream like liquid Val-
ium. I experience this when I find my father dancing impulsively in
front of a car near some army barracks during World War II, with a
rolled-up newspaper in his hand; he waves it like a wand. Or is he con-
ducting? Haydn on the car radio? On the back of the photograph he
wrote "Williamsburg's answer to Fred Astaire," meaning for the
photo to be sent home. I itch to poeticize the moment. But whereas
Atget seems to have taken the portraits that most of the photo poems

are based on, my own photographs seem, at times, more like outtakes from Weegee or Arbus, occasionally grotesque, frequently absurd. This is not meant as a lament. Many snaps are so bland, so benign, the poses so familiar that, although they stir the memory, they are not in themselves memorable. I marvel that people are so stiffly uncommitted when photographed, so unconcerned with their presentation of self. Most of us will be seen photographically beyond the memory of anything we do, beyond even our names. I have a shot of my great-grandfather surrounded by his daughters. It was taken around the turn of the century. His beard is long, his look severe. That is all, more or less, I see in him. I could engage in speculation about his attitude or dress, but that would be based on sociological, historical, or cultural generality. I know his last name, Broslovsky, but neither I nor anyone else living remembers his first name, his occupation, or demeanor. Other than a genetic legacy, he has vanished. What remains is his visage: the stiff deportment affected in photographs of the time, nothing else. Were he aware of that withering knowledge of his limited posterity, would he have acted iconically, to preserve his distinction? Would we? The result would be self-caricature. For all I know he could be doing just that. The representative, the typical, is not necessarily memorable.

For much of my childhood I was obese. According to some of the pictures, I was not only fat, but quite a little maniac. There is a rather substantial genre of photographs that show me in various stages of attack: dressed as the devil attacking my Superman brother, as a Green Beret beatifically poised with machete, a Southern sheriff pose: rifle crossed on my chest, the holstered outlaw coolly shooting at the camera. In one shot I am astride my brother, hands high and clenched tight, with a growling smirk of Hun-like victoriousness. It is difficult to lyricize one's childhood in the face of such alienating, albeit amusing, evidence. I look at these pictures and am confronted with a disjunction of memory: I remember myself as a shy, if precociously sarcastic, child, not at all showy or hammy. But I am forced to remember that these photos were all taken by my mother, the constant other in the pictures. How often we consign the amateur photographer to oblivion, forgetting that these home stills catch us between two audiences, poised between future and present, tense with that duality. If we do not completely remember that the photo has a future, it is because we are

Family photograph by Arbus?
Why is my mother smiling at Churchill's grave?

Who is that boy?

Perfectly 1961:
Paradise lost?

The law won.

*Documenting
your descent.*

My mother's photographic transformation: 1938 (left), 1943 (below), 1948 (above).

Personal History — the paper tells of an appeal to the last caller of Marilyn Monroe.

The photographer's cruelty, or lovely indifference?

To hell with the photograph.

unable to deny the present, the photographic moment. Getting back to my photographic militarism, I can imagine that aggression, but I cannot remember it, and part of that may be due to the schizophrenia induced by my teenage weight loss. The before and after shots are radically different, but not only in a physical sense. For several years, in the A.D. photographs (after diet, at fourteen), I show a dark self-consciousness, a brooding quality. My face strains to drain itself of emotion, as though attempting inscrutability, *tabula rasa*, as though I were attempting to wipe out the past and the photographs with it. There is a gruesome sadness in these pictures, a desperation. I am an open book of attempted closure reacting to the earlier pictures, seeing in them a lack of dignity. I looked at the same photographer, and defended myself and my image against the possibility of an undignified reproduction. This played right into the hands of mine enemy, the parental myth-makers. I confirmed the family folklore that my diet had shed happiness along with skin. Caught between the camera and a hard place, I failed in my battle against interpretation: "Here is the evidence: look at the idyllic bond as you sit on your mother's lap, enraptured in a kiss; and here your frisky delight as you point the gun at her, and there your fall into thinness and resentment, the document of your descent." My captions, my photographic narrative was quite different: note how early I cover my body while trying to claim my mother's, note the photographs of my mother as an equally chubby child in some poses remarkably similar to mine, the father-taken shot of me behind bars at Universal Studio, the kiss, the attempted composure, added up to a story about self-preservation and a severing of oedipal attachment, extraordinary family catharses, emotional bloodbaths. My military poses were war games, the playful aggression a reaction to a bonding of perverse closeness. My attempted coup de grace in this historiographical war was the picture of myself, napping on the porch, baby bottle in hand at the age of three and a half. But this was where the stalemate was most fully revealed in mutual cognitive dissonance: the other camp saw what had been my peculiar and self-contained retardation, my failure at self-weaning. Aghast, I would click shut at high speed.

I look at these photos now and feel far from nostalgic. What I know, have learned from them, is important and alienating, alienating because the evidence is so mutable. Part of me still looks back at the snaps searching for the smoking gun, the moment that clinches the prima facie case. However, what the case may be is equally ephemeral, utterly elusive, as though I've misplaced memory's fixer, its stop bath. I feel as though there should be answers, but am frequently confounded by what the questions might be.

Perhaps for that reason I have frequently delighted in showing off my photos. It is one of my rituals of intimacy. Faced with the difficulties of interpretation, I call in amenable audiences who can appreciate incongruities without having to understand them. I displace the obligations of audience from myself to my guest who, in fact, has no such obligation. The "other" in the picture, the photographer, fades into an invisible hand, replaced by the exhibitor.

I have a travel bag full of photographs and three photograph albums. The albums are the inexpensive kind with clear covers on top of the pages and sticky stuff on the surface. One album has pictures of my grandparents and my parents from their childhood to the first few years of their marriage. It ends with a few snapshots from my early childhood. The second album covers me, roughly between the ages of twenty-two and twenty-five. Why are these two periods albumized? I believe because they are the periods in my life that call out least for constant reinterpretation.

When one looks at albums, time is discrete, in geographical or chronological units, moments run together with the rhythm of polysyndeton, the passage of time forcing an organization: my grandfather wore a vest in a park in Kiev, and he walked down a street in Lakewood, New Jersey, with my grandmother, and my father posed with his siblings in the facade of a boat called the Mayflower in Coney Island, 1930, and my father danced in front of a barracks in Arizona during World War II, and my mother, in her high school graduation gown, laughed on the roof of an apartment building in Flatbush, her gown flying up in the wind, and they all beamed at my parents' wedding, my mother's silk train going on forever. These arrangements give life meaning, the individual photos all pointing forward to future arrangements. And someone begat Max who begat Rhoda who begat David.

The family album really begins with the birth of the album's owner. The first shot of him or her is a photographic exclamation mark. With it, we leave the exposition and start the rising action. Every photograph leading up to one's birth is contextually subordinate. These albums are like the biographies I used to read as a child, each moment of the past a portent of future greatness, every moment of Abraham Lincoln's grandmother's life leading up to Sumter and Gettysburg. We reveal this in the way we talk about photographs: "That was my mother and father two years before I was born." Or we use other moments of drama to delineate our lives.

However, albums, the conventional narrative form of photo showing, interest me less than grabbing from the bag, pulling out photos as though birthing successive versions of myself, offering presentations that are nonlinear, full of contrast and contradiction. The album presents the past as a golden age, a faded millennium, and presumes a progression toward . . . a second coming? At least a moment of metaphysical culmination: And Here I Am Today, the great photographic I Am. When I pick from the bag, time becomes relative. Everyone living, everyone dead, the sequence of memory is a vaudeville show, a carnival. I think of myself as Winnie, in Beckett's *Happy Days*, trying to fit together pieces of an arcane riddle, the solution to which is completely elusive and somehow hilarious. Time diffuses, moments seem to merge, connections suggest themselves, specious and tantalizing. I serve, offer this up to new coconspirators. The appetizer: I am in a girlish pose, one hand to head, one to the hip, a twist of the body, a smile alluring enough to set any pederast on edge. I am four or so. Next: three years later. I stand in front of a motel in Washington wearing a visor, holding a yellow balloon, my feet are spread at right angles, my stomach bulges beneath a blue sport shirt, spills down over brown slacks. I look tremendously pleased with myself. But it couldn't have been my salad days. The main course is a diversion. We go back to the age of three. It is a shot of my family, my parents, brother, and myself. We are on a cruise ship, the last American cruise ship to go to Cuba, as it happens. I am three. We are surrounded by a bouquet of paper flowers, with wax roses springing from the bottom. The picture is poorly cropped: my legs dangle on the lower right; someone is walking away. My mother smiles sexily, holding my brother who is holding his mouth, who looks like he is trying to mold her expression on his own face. But he has ended up sullen, and his eyes seem to hate the photographer. My father holds me, looks at me with pure affability. And I am so clever and coy. I purse my lips; I pout. I am full of consternation. I am even sexier than my mother. I don't recall ever seeing my mother looking so "come hither." My father became affable several years ago. I attempt "coy" from time to time, but it is never effective, coming out shy, or enigmatic instead. My brother? Well, he is a little sullen at times, but only when work wears him down, or the family, the three men who remain of it, clashes. There is an enormous Swiss cheese on a table to my mother's left, a conveniently ironic comment on the idyllic intentions of the portrait, the framing plastic bouquet.

This leaves us laughing, and we indulge in an aperitif: I sit on my father's lap, my fly is open, and I am pulling away, snarling so it seems. My father is angry, gripping me. My mother sits placidly at his side, hands folded between her legs. We are by a pool somewhere. Is my father angry because my fly is open? How do I reconcile the fact that my first response to this photograph is always that I wish I had my father's shirt? And my second to note unfairly, the incongruity of the placid mother, hands dangling between open legs, and the snarling father. And what did I do?

I have no idea, and it isn't really important unless I decide that it is revealing. The unruly child? The cantankerous father? The oblivious mother? None of these holds. I could link it with the girlish pose and the pursed lips. The Randy Infant? I think not.

Why is it funny? Because I am not a victorious Hun, or a small Tab Hunter. Because even if it is atypical, even if it is thirty-five years ago, it admonishes my adult composure, control of the public self. It says at least this is a dramatic moment. It tweaks the placid nose of years of pictures, of calm deportment. It says, "To hell with the photograph! I want to go swimming! I want something!" It is funny because it suggests things it cannot be saying. The same is true of the picture of my toy fox terrier, in a seemingly precarious position on the top step of the metal staircase leading to our backyard. Her head is dramatically turned back toward the camera. She seems forlorn, suicidal. She is therefore a strange and memorable dog.

Not all of my pictures are this amusing. I have a photograph of my mother, head swaddled in a kerchief, grimacing in disgust or anticipation of pain, about to apply Oil of Olay to the walnut-sized tumor on her neck. I took this one. I look at it and try to remember back to my motives for taking it. Understanding that her death was near, wanting a few last images? Was it guilt-inspired morbidity, the preservation of pain? It is in the bag with the others. As with any picture, it alters the narrative when it takes its turn. Sometimes it is a double negative, covering all the other shots, and hardly has to be drawn. Sometimes I put it back when I don't want the plot to take that turn. But it is my hedge against nostalgia, and my desire for it. In whatever sequence it comes up, it is *ubi sunt*, with a vengeance, the distillation of a paradox: a preserved moment pointing to oblivion. With my audience present, the subject becomes dominant, the photographer fades. Because of this, the loss I experience is not so distracted by both looking at the picture and through the lens at the same time.

Maybe my friend is tired now. Perhaps, as luck would have it, the final selection is a picture in front of a cage. My arms are crossed; I am cross. An elephant is on its way inside, tail swinging in the distance. I display my discontent for posterity, for my mother. I remember this moment, forty years ago, that happiness settled in a few minutes later. We went and talked to the monkeys. But I was aware that the evidence of my unhappiness remained. I wanted another picture, a chance to cancel out the earlier one, but there was no more film. I knew that I would have a lot of explaining to do. Why was I unhappy? I believe I did not want my picture taken. Too young for irony, I inspired it. I couldn't have known that the context of my unhappiness would continually shift, that the moment, calling out like a found object with the nature of a changeling, could be explained only so far.

After, we went to see the monkeys.

Some Images: Toward a Photographic Mishnah

To begin with, some images: they are the author's treat to himself. . . . And, as it happens, only the images of my youth fascinate me.

—Roland Barthes, *Roland Barthes*

We confuse the habitation of two or more people in a photographic frame with the idea that a moment, having become iconicized, is also communally experienced. Photographic coupling, however, is nothing more than divergent contiguities bedfellowed by a movement of the finger, ending with a click. "Do you remember when we went to the ocean," we say, looking at a photograph, as though *ocean* were a mnemonic noodle two subjects could simultaneously suck in, ending face to face. It is only when memory is darker, perhaps more desperately disputed, that we ask, "What did you think was happening?" We might as well, we could as well, spend our lives asking that question, of others or ourselves. "But, gentle strawperson," you might ask, "couldn't you spend your life trying to interpret experience, and neglect experiencing it?" In the memory business, this is known as the experiential, definitional end run, posing life as what we do when we aren't trying to understand what anything means. In families, the age of innocence is the age of unreflection. Colloquially, this is called nostalgia, and it is always posthumous; we resist the fall into a hermeneutics of the self, and justify our resistance as fear of narcissism. In the photograph, I (far right) have just explained all of this in exactly these terms. My father is delighted at my precociousness. My brother is skeptical. My mother sarcastic. The photographer is performing the dance of the four veils; he owes it to us; his composition is heartfelt, but sloppy. Were they all alive, I feel certain my family would have come around to confirming everything I have said.

If the shadow of the photographer is in the left foreground, my father must have served in the Third Theater on Mars. What is that stovepipe head-shaped thing, looming? What is the dance with a rolled-up newspaper that men do in uniforms? Or is he playing the violin? First Sergeant, First Violin. The unrestrained happiness of parents in old photographs is unbearable, perhaps because of our bitterness at who they became for us, our desire to connect only with their younger selves, who would understand our grievances. Unbearable photographs: the shadows the subjects are unaware of that we must bear for them in our photopyrrhic victories of hindsight. My father fiddles while I burn.

The other day I was talking to my father and I made a joke about Luna Park, the amusement park next to Coney Island which, in my childhood, made extraordinary progress: from desultory to defunct. My father asked me what I had been up to, something like "What have you been doing, you little fuck?" I believe I said, "None of your fucking business. Skipping school to go to Luna Park." His response was delightedly taken aback, the kind I am accustomed to eliciting when I mention something I know he knows and I know he doesn't know I do (and incidentally, why is it that we so love those know-didn't-know-knew locutions?): "What do you know from Luna Park?" He was born in Williamsburg, in 1919, whereas I can claim a Coney Island pedigree, circa '57. Therefore: this picture impinges: In 1927, Luna Park, and Coney Island generally, had not yet become the kitsch downer I grew up with. This group of first-generation kids, twenty years removed from shtetl and pogrom, are ensconced in a fading but not yet faded piece of Americana. How strange to think their world was unironically brave and new. My father must be eight, on the Mayflower. I am now forty-five, in a college town in the Midwest. People say, "You don't sound like you're from New York." I feel pleased. And I feel queasy, as though those painted waves were being smudged by my stubby little fingers. Yes, no, I never skipped school to go to Luna Park. I was busy reading about its heyday, when millions were amused, and abstractly measuring my distance from it. How does a ridiculous sign of pride coexist with a sublime sense of loss? This photograph is innocent, if anything is. And I have decided that innocence should not be an analytical category. Therefore, I renounce my claim on Coney Island.

I am the photographer of vertigo-dog. The moment before the second suicide attempt. She did it so it felt real. She had faced our featureless Jew linen. You have driven me to this, she seems to be saying. Psychologically, pets are tormented by the cultural distance they experience from their masters. And amateur photographs are dramatized moments whose perspectives are most frequently accidental. Nevertheless, the photograph inhabits the realm of dramatic reality, and is, of course, no less absurd for this. And no less true that she turned, and I snapped. And no less true that after her plunge I stood at the edge, looking down, with arms extended while the mission bells sounded.

I can hardly stand to look at this snapshot. Three months after I ended my life as an endomorph. I am closing my eyes as if trying to understand new sensations of physical space. The hand is almost in the pocket. The body seems to press out, to show the ghost, the phantom of its lost burden, the pounds of flesh. The upper torso floats above the trees, the lower poised between garbage pails. I am the mind/body problem. There is a will to be otherwise, otherwheres, in the eyes. The smile a well-practiced enigma. This is me as Mona Lisa.

1962 in the Catskills. In a photograph taken the day before, my grand-mother sits on a lawn chair, a newspaper draped on her knee, while I lean into her facing the camera. Turning my grandmother and me up-side down, the *Daily News* headline emerges: "Appeal to MM's Secret Caller." Marilyn Monroe has just died. The personal and political en-gage in a complex transaction when you know, more or less, where you were when Monroe died.

Here, I am all cheesecake. The pocketbook in the background is an odd feature of the landscape, echoing my pose: one handle up, one down. I would row around the islands in the lake with my grandfather: my first distinct experience of silence. Back on shore, the re-entry into culture. I'm a child tart. The little lady of the lake, which has the dis-junctive dreaminess of Atget in Versailles.

I used to leave this photograph out to show my feminine side, not bothering to explain that my coy exhibitionism was murdered, or merely died, shortly thereafter, certainly sometime before 1964.

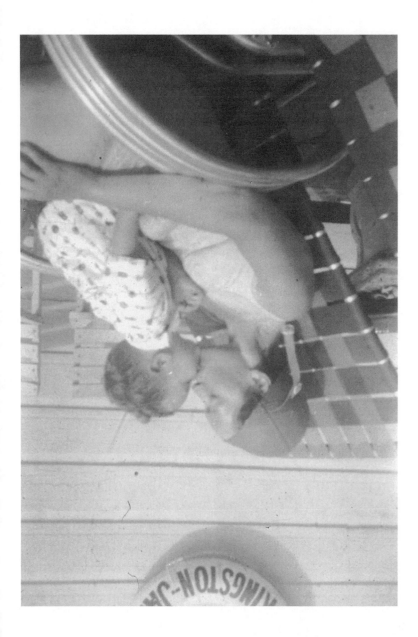

CALLING DR. FREUD! What can I say? I remember sitting in the bathroom after a bath, my brother and mother on the floor, I sitting on the toilet seat while my mother dried me off. I kissed my mother over and over on the lips. Long smacks. My brother looked disgusted. He said, "You two are disgusting," and walked out. This was my victory. The downside: a primal, first experience of shame. Kissing begins in my memory with this photograph, on a cruise ship to Jamaica, Haiti, and Cuba, in 1959. *The Kiss*. We embody the Rodin lovers. There is a comical version of Munch's *Scream* in a corner of the photograph. Only I can see it. I wish my fingers could still curl with delight. But that was in another country, and besides we were at sea.

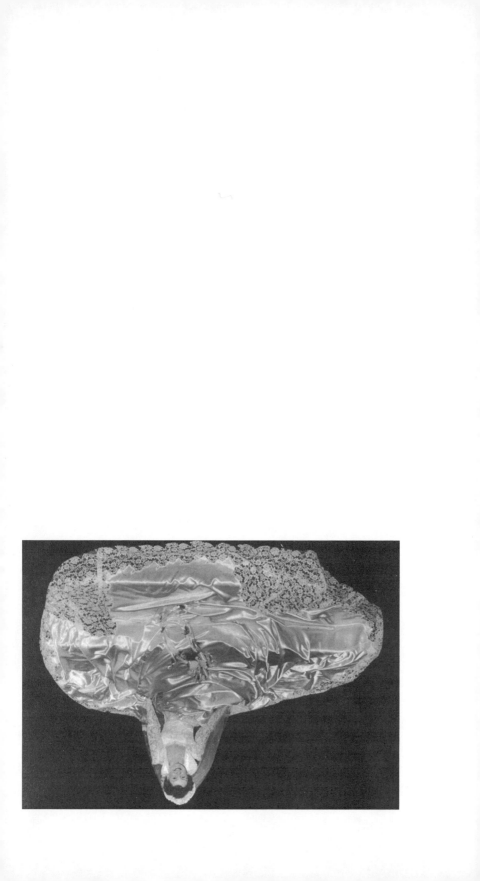

Surrounded by a darkness to which she has returned.
The effect is dramatic, indeed. The white satin shimmers undistractedly. The young face shimmers undistractedly. How dark was the room, I wonder. How bright the flash? My mother floats in a world that presents her in pure brideliness. Extra virgin. Or as Popeye sang to Olive Oyl, "A wimmin's a mystery all through history."

Is the bride here reduced to the exaltation of her role? Who can deny the power of an apotheosized moment? Nevertheless, the young woman is nothing less than happy.

How ironic, then, how unfortunate that this virgin is my *Mater Dolorosa*.

Sightline Books
The Iowa Series in Literary Nonfiction